MW00856611

How to Build a Billion Dollar Company from Scratch. . .

An Entrepreneurial Handbook:

How to Build a Billion Dollar Company from Scratch

by Harry E. Figgie Jr.

with Adam Snyder

Editorial Director: Susan Slack
Design Director: Emily Korsmo, Ruder Finn Design
Production Director: Valerie Thompson
Digital Imaging Specialist: Steve Moss

ISBN 10: 1-932646-46-9
ISBN 13: 978-1-932646-46-7

Printed in China

Foreword

JOEL L. REED, Principal, RA Capital Group

HARRY FIGGIE GREW UP IN 1930s Cleveland. He lost his father in 1940 at the age of sixteen, and five years later was fighting in General Patton's Third Army with an infantry division in Europe. After coming home, he finished his last two years of undergraduate work with a Bachelor's in metallurgical engineering. Next he received an MBA from Harvard as a member of the Class of 1949, which Larry Shames, in his 1974 book, called "the most wildly successful batch of MBAs to have shared a campus anywhere, ever."[1] Along the way, Harry also accumulated a law degree and a masters in industrial engineering by going to night school while working full time in sales and in manufacturing positions.

From 1953 until 1962 Harry worked at the consulting firm, Booz Allen Hamilton. While becoming a partner and later a subsidiary president, he became one of the country's leading cost reduction experts. In 1963, after gaining more operating experience as a group vice president of A.O. Smith, he went out on his own and took over the Automatic Sprinkler Corporation of America, a struggling $23 million sprinkler company. He spent the next thirty years turning it into a $1.3 billion, consistently profitable, diversified corporation.

Harry Figgie has already written a best-seller, *Bankruptcy 1995*, in which he warns America of the dangers of high deficits and

1 Two books were actually written about the 1949 HBS class—*The Big Time; The Harvard Business School's Most Successful Class & How It Shaped America* by Laurence Shames, Harper Collins, 226 pages, 1986 and *Kindred Spirits: Harvard Business School's Extraordinary Class of 1949 and How they Transformed American Business* by David Callahan, John Wiley & Sons, 320 pages, 2002.

profligate government spending. It sold more than 300,000 copies and was on the *New York Times* bestseller list for almost a year. He is also the author of the successful *Cost Reduction and Profit Improvement Handbook* that teaches executives the straightforward management techniques that made Automatic Sprinkler's successor company, Figgie International, so successful.

Harry has also had his share of heartache. In mid 1992 he fell seriously ill and was bedridden for fifteen months. Figgie International's interim management proceeded to spend $70 million on consultants. Within two years the company was in dire financial straits. That's when I first met Harry. His departure from the company left him in an unfamiliar role—that of a shareholder, not an operator, of his beloved Figgie International, which continued to under perform. Harry wanted someone to assist him in redirecting the company. But this time it would have to be done from the outside.

Harry, one of the quickest studies I've ever come across, absorbed the philosophy and execution steps associated with "shareholder activism" and applied it to his own company. I recall his eyes lighting up like a child's upon discovering this wondrous new technique. Harry succeeded in his mission to improve Figgie International's share price by applying many of the same traits that had made him a winner as an operator.

As more projects provided opportunities to work with Harry, I began to appreciate his remarkable talents. It took several years of filtering acquisition targets, watching him pour over operating results and seeing him take management to task if they failed to hit their "Hardcore" budget numbers, before I understood that his success in building companies stemmed from a highly disciplined process.

Now, for the first time, this book provides the roadmap to that process; one that has proven successful and is every bit as relevant to today's entrepreneurs. It's a process that made Harry Figgie one of the leading builders of companies in America.

This is not just a "How To" book. It is the story of Harry Figgie, a man who combined intelligence, judgment, tenacity, discipline and hard work toward building a billion dollar company from scratch. Like any true entrepreneur, he has had his ups and downs—but he never stays down. Flanked by his remarkably talented wife Nancy, and his very capable sons, Harry still relishes a good challenge … which he approaches with the disciplined process that the reader is about to discover.

—Joel L. Reed
February, 2008

TIMELINE

Growth of Figgie International, Inc.

December 31, 1963
Purchase of Automatic Sprinkler Corporation of America

November 17, 1968
Company goes public

1964
Sales go from $22.7 million to $25.2 million and profits from $334,000 to $1,116,000.

October 30, 1969
Name change to A-T-O, Inc.

1965 – 1969
Acquires 51 companies, increasing total sales from $22.7 million to $379 million

1970 – 1985
Internal growth from $356 million to $721 million

May 20, 1981
Name change to Figgie International, Inc.

1985 – 1990
Acquires 38 companies, increasing total sales from $803 million to $1.3 billion

Introduction

WITH THE HELP OF A SMALL GROUP of likeminded individuals, between 1963 and 1987 we turned a $23 million fire sprinkler company into a $1.3 billion diversified public corporation. There is no reason someone could not do the same thing today. In fact, it could be done in a lot less time than 25 years because it's so much easier today to obtain financing.

I had a plan and we stuck to it. First an investment banker friend helped me put together $7.2 million to buy the Automatic Sprinkler Corporation of America, a small fire protection company in Youngstown, Ohio. We had to cobble together bank financing, personal loans, and a giveback to the original owners of ten percent of the company in the form of a convertible preferred, known today as mezzanine financing. Mezzanine financing is a hybrid of debt and equity financing, typically used either to finance the expansion of an existing company or for a company that is expecting to go public within a year or so. We wore out the prayer rugs at the handful of banks that would even consider financing a new acquisition-minded company. This was during a period when banks weren't inclined to invest in small companies. You had to find those few willing to gamble on people.

Today it is much easier than it was then to raise funds, mainly due to the massive growth of pension funds that has fueled the proliferation of venture capital funds. But whether it's a bank or a venture capitalist, you are still going to have to convince them that they are not throwing their money away and that they will get a considerable return on their investment. Particularly venture capitalists will be looking to be left with equity control after recouping their initial investment.

Once we financed our first purchase, we used the profit improvement techniques I had learned in consulting at Booz Allen Hamilton to triple cash flow at Automatic Sprinkler to just over $1 million. That was enough to support a small corporate staff. We used tried and true methods that are just as effective today as they were then—common sense measures, like ratio analysis and work sampling, ABC inventory control, product redesign, and a focus on those areas where the company was spending most of its money.

Once Automatic Sprinkler was running smoothly, our first growth phase was accomplished by acquiring companies that fit into certain broad categories, each of which was called a nucleus. We chose growth areas like fire protection and defense, and later services like insurance and real estate. But you could just as easily focus on other business categories. We had a total of six nucleuses. In five years we purchased more than fifty companies and grew our sales from $23 million to $379 million. We did it by buying small, often struggling companies, turning them around, and then growing them. Those were the only kinds of companies we could afford. We had to hit singles and doubles, not home runs. It was a dangerous approach, but the only one open to us at that time because of limited financing opportunities.

A Few Early Guidelines for Getting Started

- Companies doing between $50 and $500 million in sales represent the backbone of the U.S. economy. That's where I would begin if I wanted to build a large, diversified public company from scratch.
- You will have to convince banks or venture capitalists that they are not throwing their money away and that they will be left with equity in your company after getting a considerable return on their investment.
- Surround yourself with people who thrive on crises, who like to grab hold of things and DO something, who have a primal impatience to get their hands around a problem and shake it around until a solution presents itself.
- Use tried and true, common sense measures to increase profits, like ratio analysis and work sampling, ABC inventory control, product redesign, and a focus on those areas where your company is spending most of its money.

I did not do it alone, of course, not by a long shot. I found good, competent, hardworking people to help me. To a great extent I think our success was attributable to handpicking a select group of people who shared my drive and vision of what we could create. In the early days at least, I seemed to have surrounded myself with people who thrived on crises. They liked to grab hold of things and DO something. They had a primal impatience to get their hands on a problem and shake it around until a solution presented itself. Today they're called entrepreneurs, although we didn't use the word back then. In those days the dictionary definition of entrepreneur was simply a person who manages. But however you define the word, if you plan on building a large company from scratch, you need to surround yourself with these kind of people.

If I were to do it all over again, I would acquire larger, healthier companies which wouldn't need a decade or more of consolidation and internal growth to gain a significant market share. Today there are more companies than ever from which to choose. In northern Ohio alone, just a few years ago more than 500 companies were doing between $50 and $500 million in sales. Even with all the megadeals in recent years, I still think these are the companies that represent the backbone of the U.S. economy, and that's where I'd begin if I wanted to build a large, diversified public company from scratch. Smaller companies of $5-$20 million in size are more difficult to grow and are generally not able to finance real growth.

After our growth by acquisition phase, we hunkered down to consolidate what we had. Still, we grew. By implementing our profit improvement program at each division, by using our nucleus theory and a strict system of annual reviews at each division, and by aggressively expanding our growth areas, we reached sales of $803 million in 1985, with a pretax profit of almost $50 million. During those fifteen years of internal growth, less than one percent of it came from acquisitions. Then we opened up our acquisitions again and reached sales of $1 billion in 1987 and $1.3 billion in 1989.

At our 1987 President's Meeting I announced to the division presidents that I was giving all of us five years before initiating a plan to shrink the company down to our ten largest divisions, each of which would have at least $50 million in sales, plus two growth divisions. We had twenty-three divisions at the time. I planned to use the proceeds from selling off our other divisions to pay down debt. By the end of 1993, this would have left us lean and healthy, ready to grow again within the industries we had identified. Unfortunately, I never had the opportunity to follow through on the plan. In July 1992 I fell ill and was bedridden for fifteen months. By the time I returned, the company had gone in a completely different direction.

It was a wild ride from $19 million to $1.3 billion. I am pleased to try to pass along some of our experiences and the rules I have tried to live by, not always successfully.

CHAPTER ONE

Get Ready

AFTER WAITING AN HOUR at the Yale Club in Manhattan I had to come to grips with the obvious. My friend, Dale Coenen, was not going to show.

It was uncharacteristic of Dale. Something important must have delayed him. Perhaps we had had a misunderstanding about the time. Whatever the reason, I was on my own, having arrived from Cleveland on an overnight train.

I took a deep breath and looked at the three strangers across the breakfast table in a final attempt to size them up before trying to convince them to invest almost a million dollars in a plan to take a struggling $23 million sprinkler company and quickly make it profitable enough to serve as the cornerstone of a much larger, multi-divisional corporation. But I wasn't trying to fool anyone. When it came right down to it, I was asking them to invest almost a million dollars in me.

Dale and I had been working around the clock for the past week, ever since the Automatic Sprinkler Corporation of America had been brought to my attention on December 6. 1963 by Morris Hartman, executive vice president of the Central National Bank in Cleveland. Because of a $1.7 million tax loss carry forward that would expire on December 31, the owners had given us a deadline of the end of the year, now just twelve days away, to put together a $7.2 million package to buy the company. That may seem like small change today, but it was the equivalent of more than $40 million in today's dollars, and we were trying to raise it at a time when venture capital money and pension funds as we know them today did not exist.

Getting Ready

In a sense, I had been waiting for this moment most of my life, since as a teenager I first formulated a plan to emulate what Colonel Willard Rockwell, one of my father's early business associates, had done in building Rockwell International. I was fortunate to grow up in a middle class family in Lakewood, Ohio, a Cleveland suburb, with a terrific public school system that excelled in both academics and sports. It was one of only two school districts in the area to regularly send its graduates to the Ivy League.

My mother had been a school teacher; my father worked his way through college by holding down two jobs while playing semi-professional baseball on weekends. Dad had success in the automotive parts business as a rare combination of engineer and sales executive. He was in on the founding of companies that eventually became Eaton and Rockwell, two of the larger diversified companies of that era. In the thirties, he developed a number of innovations, including the bumper guard, the gravel deflector, the wraparound bumper, and various improvements in automobile springs.

My mother and father instilled in me the idea that with hard work and focus, anything was possible in America. Whenever someone told me what I was trying to do was impossible, I remembered my parents' confidence in me and in America, and I put my head down and burrowed forward, ignoring the naysayers.

At first I thought I'd be a professional baseball player. Growing up in Lakewood, Ohio in the 1930s, I admired Lou Gehrig, Ty Cobb, and Babe Ruth, although my favorite was Charlie Gehringer, the Detroit second baseman. But by the time I was sixteen, the year my father died, my heroes had become businessmen—not only my father, but also Colonel Rockwell, who worked with my dad in the 1920s at Standard Parts Inc.[2], a manufacturer of springs and bumpers for the fledgling automobile industry.

2 The forerunner of Eaton Manufacturing

Those involved in the early years of the automobile parts industry considered Rockwell one of their own, and I followed his career as if he were a local baseball phenom. His prowess at building large companies by acquiring a series of smaller ones was legendary. After making his mark by patenting a new bearing system for truck axles, in 1953 Rockwell merged a number of companies, including Wisconsin Axle Company, Timken-Detroit Axle Company, and the Standard Steel Spring Company into the Rockwell-Standard Corporation, which quickly became one of the country's largest suppliers of automobile parts. Simultaneously he was building the Rockwell Manufacturing Company into the world's leading supplier of measurement and control equipment for fluid products. Eventually, he combined the companies he controlled into Rockwell International.

Getting Ready in a Hurry

On the evening of June 13, 1940 I woke up to find my father dying of a heart attack. Antibiotics have long since eliminated rheumatic fever in America, but my father had had it as a youngster. Back then no one understood that it often led to heart damage and premature death.

My Dad had always dreamed I would play professional baseball, and the year after he died, as a pitcher during my senior year of high school, I led the City of Cleveland in strikeouts. In the fall of 1941, I enrolled in Dartmouth's five-year business and engineering course, primarily to play ball for Jeff Tesreau, who had pitched for John McGraw's New York Giants as one of the famous four. In 1914 Tesreau had won twenty-six games for the Giants.

As it turned out, I never felt very comfortable at Dartmouth. The students were different from what I was used to. I remember one group of four kids cutting a deck of cards for a buck a cut. That bothered me. A dollar was really worth something back then—in 1941 the average annual salary in the United States was just over $2,000! It's not in my nature to spend frivolously, something which I took to heart in my personal life, but also in my approach to running a public company and to the way I hoped the federal government would operate. No doubt I inherited my fiscal sobriety from my parents. My father's family came to Cleveland from Switzerland in 1869 and my Mom reportedly was descended from a well known English inventor. The other side of her family can be traced to 1669 Rhode Island.

Two months after I started at Dartmouth the Japanese attacked Pearl Harbor and everyone's life changed. I knew it was only a matter of time before I'd be in the service, and felt I should be closer to home. I also wanted to pursue a curriculum that focused more on engineering and business, as opposed to the more heavily liberal arts courses Dartmouth had to offer. Dad always taught me that if you knew how to build something, and you knew how to sell it, you would always have a job. This was during the depression, so having a job was of paramount concern to everyone. I kept his advice in mind while making decisions about my education and professional choices.

Surviving World War II

During the summer of 1942 I transferred to Case Institute of Technology, but a year later I turned down an engineering deferment and enlisted in the Army. In early 1945 I found myself crossing the Atlantic as part of the 86th Infantry Division, sleeping on the bottom bunk in the lowest deck of a converted German luxury liner. The winter weather prevented anyone from staying on deck for long, and we spent the voyage alternating between feeling nauseous and actually being sick. Latrine duty consisted of making sure the next guy in line didn't hit his head when he was throwing up.

I ended up in an infantry division in Patton's Third Army. During the worst of the fighting I constantly thought of how my parents had always talked to me about the importance of family, and that I was all that remained of the Figgie name. If I died, my line died, something I didn't want to happen but over which I had little control.

I would guess that most everyone who survived combat has similar stories, but I still shake my head at some of the close calls. One afternoon I was crossing an open field and heard what we called incoming mail, in this case German 88 artillery shells. There was no place to take cover, so I just dove down flat on the open ground. Four shells landed close to me—two near my feet and two near my head. All of them failed to explode. The six that landed just behind and in front of me did explode, making a tremendous sound that shook the ground. I later read in one of Stephen Ambrose's books that the reason so many shells were duds was that they were manufactured by Polish prisoners who were purposely sabotaging them. But still, four duds sandwiched between six explosions was remarkably fortunate.

Once the war in Europe was over, my division was scheduled for the first invasion of Japan, in November 1945. I am one of those thousands of guys whose life President Truman saved by dropping the two atomic bombs. One of my buddies in intelligence later told me that my division had been scheduled for one hundred percent casualties within the first two days of an invasion. I am pleased to be able to write this book sixty years later.

I returned from the battlefield with one overriding feeling—I was incredibly lucky to be alive. I couldn't shake the feeling that the Lord had saved me for something, that I had a destiny. I think a lot of us felt that way.

I also brought home more tangible souvenirs, including some one million German mark notes, rendered worthless by the Weimar Republic's prewar inflation. This stark reminder of how inflation can ravage a country would remain with me all my life. It is no doubt the genesis of a number of projects I've been involved with, including my bestselling book, *Bankruptcy 1995*, published by Little Brown and Company in 1992, that warned of the inflationary consequences of unchecked government spending. It would be as if I showed you a U.S. million dollar bill and a half million dollar bill. There are people who say it can't happen. I have currency from Germany that indicates it can.

Getting Educated

Back home after the war I used the GI Bill to reenroll at Case Institute of Technology. Taking both day and night classes, I received my engineering degree in metallurgy in a total of five and a half semesters spread out before and after the War. In the fall of 1947 I entered Harvard Business School as a member of the now well-publicized Class of 1949. Its alumni include a U.S. Congressman, an SEC Chairman, and the heads of at least a dozen Fortune 500 companies. More than a quarter of the class retired as CEOs or presidents of their respective companies.

At the time, Harvard was the only school in the United States offering a two-year MBA program. I was immediately struck by the seriousness of most of my classmates, in stark contrast to some of my previous college experiences. Most of us were veterans, and the war had made us appreciate what we had.

"Nothing ever happens until you sell something."
—Arthur (Red) Motley, publisher

Harvard was an eye opener in a number of ways. Using the case method, our professors taught us to look at the big picture when analyzing a company's performance and potential. I still remember the first day, the professor passing out a case study and telling us to construct a pro forma P & L and balance sheet. I had a metallurgical engineering degree, and I knew a number of different ways to kill someone with a bayonet, but I had no idea what a pro forma P & L and balance sheet was. For an engineer, this was an entirely new world.

Two visiting lecturers made a particular impression on me. Arthur (Red) Motley was an entrepreneur's entrepreneur, having started a company at the age of thirteen from his family's farm to sell topsoil and manure to his neighbors. He told us that nothing ever happens until you sell something[3], and demonstrated how he had used that notion as editor of *Parade* magazine to build its circulation until it was the nation's largest weekly publication.

"Build something you believe in and you will create something of value."
—Margaret Rudkin, founder, Pepperidge Farm

The other visiting entrepreneur I remember was Margaret Rudkin, the founder of Pepperidge Farm. She started that company in 1937 after her family doctor suggested her son's asthma would be helped

3 Motley is also credited with saying, "If the nation's economists were laid end to end, they would point in all directions."

if she baked her own wheat bread. Just like Colonel Rockwell, she told us that if we patiently built something we believed in, we would create something of value. I took that advice to heart.

My Smartest Decision

During the summer after my first year at Harvard I made the smartest, most important decision of my life. My mother always told me that "you can get all the education and experience you want, but it is the woman you marry who will make or break you." Fortunately for me, I've had a lifelong partner in Nancy Furst. We met in 1948 on a blind date set up by my friend, Bud Chockley, who had been captured in the Battle of the Bulge and spent some time in a prisoner of war camp. I was the best man at his wedding, and he later was the best man at mine.

Nancy was a junior at Northwestern University, where she was president of her sorority and of Mortar Board, the women's national honor society. Joe Miller, the University's dean of student affairs, told me she was the biggest BWOC (big woman on campus) ever to attend Northwestern.

Before proposing I explained to Nancy what I wanted to do with my life, to eventually have my own small company and build it into a larger one. She told me she thought "I was nuts, but let's go." We were married on August 20, 1949.

> Get experience at a small division of a medium size company, a medium size division of a large company, and a large division of a large company.

Have a Plan

I think it's important to have a plan. That doesn't mean you have to know what you want to do with the rest of your life at the age of sixteen. But too many businessmen just react to events as they occur rather than trying to create their own events that react to their hopes and dreams. As someone who recently celebrated his eighty-fourth birthday, I can tell you it all goes by extremely fast. Who said life is what happens to you when you're busy making other plans? I think it was John Lennon[4].

My plan after Nancy and I were married was to get both the experience and education I thought I'd need. I wanted to work for a small division of a medium size company, a medium size division of a large company, and a large division of a large company. I also took seriously my Dad's advice to learn how to make something and to sell it. My employment during these years included both sales and manufacturing assignments at Western Automatic Machine Screw in Detroit and Elyria, Ohio, a general superintendent job at Parker Hannifin, and finally back in Detroit with Firestone Steel Products selling jet engine parts and automotive stampings.

At the start of the Korean War, Western Automatic Machine Screw transferred me from Detroit to its plant in Elyria, just twenty miles from my home in Lakewood. I began attending two night schools simultaneously, one to get a Masters in Industrial Engineering from Case Institute of Technology, and another for a law degree from Cleveland Marshall. I thought both degrees would be helpful for building my own company.

I never expected to practice law, but at Harvard several of my professors told me that as a businessman, it would be extremely helpful to understand it. One of them slammed down a huge stack of papers on his desk and told us with a flourish, "Gentlemen, in your careers you're going to have a pile of new laws from Congress at least this high, and if you include all the administrative regulations it will touch the ceiling. You'll be governed by all of them."

I felt the same thing about industrial engineering. If I was going to build a company, I would need to understand the rapid advancements that were being made on the manufacturing floor. Since I had all but used up my GI Bill benefits, to pay for night school I taught industrial procurement and marketing at Cleveland College, then part of Western Reserve University.

Nancy made it all possible. She held down her own advertising job and still found time to type my school papers and masters thesis and attend my Monday and Wednesday night law classes

4 From the song, *Beautiful Boy* by John Lennon

when I was working out of town. On weekends we would review her notes. To this day Nancy says she can close her eyes and picture my masters thesis, and the frustration of a typo on the last line of a page that would force her to crumple it up and begin it again. The content of that thesis was later adapted by the National Screw Machine Products Association as their official preventive maintenance program for multiple spindle screw machinery.

> In order to achieve the same profit improvement realized through a 10% reduction in costs, sales would have to almost triple.
>
> Working as a consultant or for a venture capital firm investigating startups and helping some of them grow are great ways to prepare for running your own company.

Cutting Costs as the Best Way to Improve Profits

I had already followed my father's advice and learned how to make something and to sell it. Now I needed to learn how to fix it, and in 1953 I began a nine-year stint at the consulting firm, Booz Allen Hamilton. It turned out to be the best experience I could possibly have to prepare me for owning my own company. By the time I went out on my own and began acquiring small, ailing businesses in need of profit improvement, I had seen virtually every problem a manufacturing company had to offer.

I think consulting is still a great way to prepare for running your own company, but today there are other ways as well. Working for a venture capital firm investigating startups and helping some of them grow is one. A venture capital or consulting firm might also drop you into a company to operate it for a time, another kind of invaluable experience.

Most of my Booz Allen assignments entailed situations in which profits had to be improved quickly. I learned that the best way to do that was to cut costs, which I found you could do by ten percent annually for at least three years in a row at virtually any company. That's still true today, but still tough to sell. Most people believe they are running a tight ship. The fact is that it can almost always be made tighter without harming the company.

But my most important lesson was that it is easier to improve profits by cutting costs than by increasing sales. Reducing costs by ten percent at a company doing $10 million in sales with a five percent pretax profit margin increases profits a whopping 190 percent—from $500,000 to $1.45 million, assuming all other factors remain stable. In order to achieve the same percentage increase through an increase in sales, volume would have to jump from $10 million to $29 million (5% of $29 million = $1.45 million)—not an impossible task, but certainly more difficult than a ten percent reduction in costs. Sales increases also have negative consequences that cost reduction does not, such as large working capital requirements that increase debt. Cost reduction is virtually free, and does not increase working capital or debt.

Improving Profits 190% by Cutting Costs 10%

Sales	Cost of Sales @ 95%	Pretax Profit	Savings from 10% Cost Reduction Program	Pretax Profits after 10% Cost Reduction Program
$10 million	$9.5 million	$500,000	$950,000	$1.45 million

> Rather than buying expensive new equipment, look first at those areas where your company is spending most of its money.

Tackle Largest Costs First

Many manufacturing companies go about cost reduction the wrong way by focusing first on areas that do not have the greatest potential for savings. One pitfall, for example, is the tendency to try to reduce operating expenses by purchasing expensive equipment. While new equipment may create some savings, it also requires significant capital investment and ongoing depreciation costs. All too often there is no payback analysis when a company purchases new equipment. If a million dollar piece of equipment saves one percent of your manufacturing costs, increasing debt and burden along the way, the equipment will be obsolete before it pays for itself. There have been great advancements in manufacturing in recent years, but you still have to concern yourself with payback.

In addition to the public company that I ran for almost thirty years, my son, Matthew, and I still operate a family company, Clark Reliance, which we often used as a sort of sounding board for the much larger public company. At the family company we have spent millions on new computer-aided equipment, but we have also been careful not to allow computers to replace our judgment. Computerized equipment can cut costs, of course, but they can also increase costs. In the first place, they are expensive, and in the second place you will need a team of knowledgeable people to run them. Quantify the savings before you make the expensive purchase. I like to see any new piece of equipment pay for itself within a year, pretax. That's a tough hurdle, but a useful measure.

The fundamental problem with relying on new equipment to improve profits is that it focuses on labor costs, which typically represent only five to ten percent of total costs and consequently is the area where manufacturing companies generally save the least. Rather than walk into a plant and immediately recommend that a company retool, use a different mindset when it comes to cost reduction. Think of it instead as profit improvement. At Booz Allen fifty years ago, in building Figgie International, and now in operating several manufacturing companies, I've learned to tackle first those areas where the largest sums of money are involved, because that is where the greatest savings can be gained. In a manufacturing operation that is almost always the materials area.

The logic is simple. If material represents forty-five percent of a company's costs, a ten percent cost reduction program can improve profits by ninety percent. That same ten percent cost reduction program aimed at direct labor, if it represents a typical eight percent of costs, will only improve profits by sixteen percent.

Improving Profits 90% by Cutting Costs 10%				
Sales	Estimated Profit @ 5%	Cost of Labor @ 8%	Savings from 10% CR Program on Labor Costs	Increase in Profit from 10% CR on Labor
$10 million	$500,000	$800,000	**$80,000**	**16%** (from $500,000 to $580,000)
Sales Costs	Estimated Profit @ 5%	Cost of Materials @ 45%	Savings from 10% CR Program on Cost of Materials	Increase in Profit from 10% CR on Materials
$10 million	$500,000	$4.5 million	**$450,000**	**90%** (from $500,000 to $950,000)

Mathematics do not change with time. The greatest savings can always be realized by cutting costs in those areas where your company is spending the most. These are also the areas that tend to require the least amount of capital spending.

It is just common sense. In fact, many of the problems I encountered while a Booz Allen consultant could be solved with common sense, eventually backed up by the experience of having seen most problems before. For example, a valve manufacturer in Ohio was losing a distributor a month because its deliveries were always late. I walked through the plant and saw that it was running short run parts on long run machines. Setup time for a long run machine, in those days something like a multiple spindle screw machine, could be anywhere from 8-30 hours, so you had to run thousands of parts on it to justify the high setup costs. A short run machine is one that is easy to set up, on which you can make a small number of parts quickly. By making the appropriate parts on the appropriate machines, we began to meet delivery dates.

In Iowa, the South Bend Tackle Company was facing bankruptcy if it couldn't get its production line straightened out so that it could ship its key seasonal orders by the end of February. At one plant we broke one of the plant's key bottlenecks by purchasing a simple cylindrical sander that eliminated having to hand sand each fishing rod individually. At another plant I sent the chief engineer to Dupont's headquarters in Delaware to have chemists there help us come up with a solution to another problem we were having—the plastic reel holders snapping in two.

Cash McCall

I had a lot of airplane time during these years, and I tried to keep abreast of the era's best-selling business books, titles like *The Organization Man* by William Whyte and *The Lonely Crowd* by David Riesman. But more popular were novels about businessmen, like *The Man in the Gray Flannel Suit* by Sloan Wilson, and *Cash McCall* by Cameron Hawley. I was particularly impressed with Cash McCall, a self-described buyer and seller of companies, making his living "by the simple process of buying a company in which someone has lost faith and selling it to someone else who could be made to have faith in it." Cash describes himself as "a dealer in secondhand companies." He said, "I buy them and sell them. When I buy a company, I usually put in someone to operate it for a time —long enough to give it a general overhauling, refurbish it, attempt to make it a more valuable property than it was when I bought it. Then I sell it at a profit."[5]

But I didn't just want to be like Cash McCall. Rather than sell improved companies at a profit, I wanted to make them part of a larger, more diversified company. At Booz Allen I discovered that I had a knack for straightening out money-losing companies, for walking into an operation and quickly understanding what had to be done to cut costs, operate it more efficiently, and increase profitability. The fictional Cash McCall made a lot of money by buying companies, straightening them out, and reselling them. For me it wasn't about the money. My hero was Colonel Rockwell. I wanted to build something.

I made my first acquisition after Booz Allen asked me to start an industrial engineering subsidiary, called Booz Allen Method Services, or BAMS, as we called it. To get it going, we bought two

5 Cash McCall by Cameron Hawley, Houghton Mifflin, 444 pages, 1955.

small industrial engineering companies, one in California that specialized in manufacturing methods and another in Atlanta that focused on office standards. Within a year BAMS had more than one hundred industrial engineers working for it.

Now I felt I had done everything I had been advised to do to prepare for purchasing my own company. I had manufacturing and sales experience. I had specialized in cost reduction and profit improvement, and now had operating experience. I had even made two acquisitions for Booz Allen.

I sought the advice of the head of the Investment Bankers Association, the father-in-law of a Booz Allen colleague. He likened what I wanted to do to "building battleships." At first he told me it couldn't be done because there was no money available to finance a strategy of building a diversified corporation through acquisitions. "Colonel Rockwell did it by getting the Mellon Bank to back him," I said. "Why couldn't I?" He laughed and told me there were actually more recent examples than Rockwell, men like Charles Bludhorn on the east coast, who was in the process of diversifying Gulf & Western, and Tex Thorton on the west coast, who was building Litton Industries. But he further suggested that I should have top operating experience before going out on my own. So when Gardner Heidrick, another former Booz Allen colleague who had started the executive recruiting agency, Heidrick & Struggles, told me there was an opening as group vice president in charge of A.O. Smith's industrial products companies, I jumped at the opportunity.

The divisions under my authority at A.O. Smith were a variety of manufacturing operations—glass-lined chemical tanks, oil and gas meters, electric motors, and welding equipment. The plants were located throughout the Midwest, and I continued to spend many weeks on the road. We consolidated operations, implemented the profit improvement techniques developed at Booz Allen, and made what I think was A.O. Smith's very first acquisition, Clark Controller. In two years the group's sales increased from $36 million to $76 million. Pretax profits went from $737,000 to $5.3 million.

A $20 million company can throw off $1 million in after tax profit, enough to impress the financial community, provide sufficient equity and cash flow for further acquisitions, and allow for the hiring of a small team of executives to help build a larger, diversified corporation.

Raising $7.2 Million

By 1963 I thought I was ready. I was looking for something quite specific, a company in the $20 million sales range that I could make into the first building block of a much larger public company. I figured that operated properly, a $20 million company could throw off $1 million in after-tax profit, enough to impress the financial community, provide sufficient equity and cash flow for further acquisitions, and allow me to hire a small team of executives to help build a larger, diversified corporation. Anything less than $20 million tended to lack the three Ms—**M**oney, **M**anagement, **M**arkets.

For the better part of the year I spread the word that I was looking for a company to purchase. On Thursday, December 5, 1963, Morris Hartman, executive vice president at the Central Bank in Cleveland, invited me to lunch to suggest three possibilities. The first was National Screw and Bolt, a well known name in the fastener industry. I knew something about that business, and knew that the Japanese were beginning to dominate the field and I didn't want any part of it. But the next company he mentioned, the Automatic Sprinkler Corporation of America, immediately peaked my interest. I never did learn the identity of the third company.

I was familiar with the sprinkler industry because Booz Allen had done some consulting work for the Rockwood Sprinkler Company in Worcester, Massachusetts. Fire protection had always struck me as a business with a lot of growth potential. Sprinkler sales in the United States were increasing about six percent per year, while the cost of fires was rising by seventeen percent. What's more, most large buildings, even schools, hospitals, and government offices, still had no sprinkler systems. I figured this would change once insurance companies made fire protection a condition of coverage and protecting people became as important as protecting goods and machinery.

Automatic Sprinkler was in my price range, but only if I acted quickly. The price was $7.2 million, $1.4 million under book value, but only if the sale could be completed before the end of the year, when the owners' $1.7 million tax loss carry forward was due to expire. That gave me seventeen working days, including Christmas week, to come up with more than $7 million.

The first thing I did was call Dale Coenen. Dale and I knew each other from our Booz Allen days, when he was working on marketing assignments in New York and Philadelphia and I was based in Cleveland, concentrating mostly on turnaround situations. By 1961 Dale had left Booz Allen to specialize in corporate finance. As an analyst at the brokerage house Kidder Peabody, he concentrated on private placement and public underwriting, and learned how to investigate companies from a financial perspective. Since early 1963 he had been doing mergers and acquisitions work for Laird and Company, a small investment banking group based in New York and Wilmington, Delaware.

At first glance Dale and I might have seemed an oddly matched pair. He was slim and dapper from the East, I was a meat and potato Midwesterner. Dale is smooth and soft spoken, while I'm a nuts and bolts kind of guy. But together we've always fed off each other, with Dale grasping the solutions to financial problems the same way I try to walk through a plant and pinpoint areas ripe for cost improvement.

On Sunday December 8, 1963, Dale and I sat in my living room surrounded by pads, pencils, financial reports, blueprints, product literature, personnel lists, property inventories and assorted handwritten notes from the flurry of phone calls we had made to bankers and other people who might be able to help us raise the $7.2 million we needed. Until well past midnight we poured over the data.

Automatic Sprinkler had been formed in May 1910 when four companies were merged and moved into a new plant in Youngstown, Ohio. In 1926 John Coakley, a former U.S. Steel vice president, took control and after his death in 1950 his eldest son John Coakley Jr. succeeded him as president. By 1963 Automatic Sprinkler was owned by a Coakley family trust, with a brother-in-law, John Power, in charge of its day-to-day operations. John was a very capable operator in the sprinkler field.

The more I learned about the company, the more I was convinced I could use it as my first building block. Sure, I knew it had problems, including an inefficient, costly sales system and high labor costs. The company tended to keep its books open until well into the new year, until it had closed enough jobs to show a small annual profit. In 1962 it had eked out a profit of one-half percent, amounting to $90,000 on sales of $19 million. The following year sales jumped to $22.7 million, but profits of just over $270,000 still only represented one and two-tenths percent of sales.

To me, these numbers represented opportunity. Automatic Sprinkler had an impressive market share within a growth industry. It was an experienced, respected company, one of the acknowledged leaders in the field, with a fire protection product I thought had a great future. The production facility in Youngstown was old, but adequate, with a trained work force and a national sales network. Over the years, Automatic Sprinkler had introduced significant product innovations, and by 1963 it was the number two sprinkler company in the United States, although a distant second to the Grinnell Corporation in Rhode Island.

As an important step toward cobbling together the $7.2 purchase price, Dale intended to ask the Coakley family to take back $1.4 million in preferred shares with warrants for a ten percent ownership in the company. I didn't think there was any way the Coakleys would agree to that, but Dale told me to let him worry about coming up with the money, and focus instead on running it once it was ours. Dale was right. Faced with losing a $1.7 million tax credit if they couldn't close a sale in the next three weeks, the Coakley family was feeling the pressure as much as we were. They agreed to our terms.

I had never heard of the phrase, but later I learned we had used "mezzanine financing," which is basically debt capital that gives the lender the right to convert to an ownership or equity interest in the company if the loan is not paid back in time and in full. It is generally subordinated to debt provided by the primary bank or other lender and offered with little or no collateral, so the return on investment is often expected to be 20 percent or higher. But mezzanine financing is advantageous to the company because it is treated like equity on the balance sheet, making it easier to obtain standard bank financing.

Now we only had to raise $5.8 million, so on Tuesday, December 10 Dale and I met with Morrie Hartman to see how much of that the Central National Bank would agree to underwrite. We also needed an additional $2 million credit line for working capital.

Dale and I left the bank without receiving a firm commitment, but I was fortunate to have another banking card to play. As a Booz Allen consultant I had helped turn around the F.C. Russell Company (Rusco), a manufacturer of storm windows in which the Union Commerce Bank in Cleveland had a large financial stake that was in serious jeopardy. People tend to remember those who help them during a crisis, and I came to the attention of George Herzog, the bank's chief executive. In 1960 the Union Commerce Bank had lent me the money to pay for my Booz Allen partnership, and a year later to buy two small companies that I still own today, Clark Manufacturing and the Reliance Gauge Column Company. I'll never forget him telling me that he never bet on assets. "I bet on people, and I'm going to bet on you," he said.

So I was confident Dale and I would receive a friendly reception at Union Commerce. I told Mr. Herzog that our first obligation was to Central National, since it had been Morrie Hartman who had brought Automatic Sprinkler to my attention in the first place. But should Central not be willing to commit to the funds we needed, I wanted to know whether we could count on the backing of Union Commerce. I spent over an hour detailing my plans for growing Automatic Sprinkler, after which Dale explained the financial package we were putting together. On a yellow legal pad Mr. Herzog wrote:

$1.0 DNI
$1.25 OK
$1.5 DE

Through his bifocals it was hard for Dale and me to tell if he was teasing us. "What does that mean?" I asked.

"DNI means that if you can only come up with $1 million in equity, the deal will be Damned Near Impossible to put together. OK means that with $1.25 million it will probably fly."

"What about DE?" I asked.

Finally George's mouth curved into a grin. "DE means that if you can come up with $1.5 million, the deal will be Damned Easy."

Now we all smiled. Dale and I left the bank with the knowledge that we had the support of the Union Commerce Bank if we could raise as little as $1.25 million. I felt very much like Cash McCall did about his banker. "And then he loaned me the money with no more security than my grandfather's reputation as an honorable man," Cash says at one point in the book.

Cleveland during these years was a harsh environment for entrepreneurs. Perhaps it didn't feel the need to encourage newcomers, since at the time Cleveland was home to many large companies, including almost two dozen on the Fortune 500 list. George Herzog was one local banker willing to take risks on young, ambitious entrepreneurs. An inspection of the litany of companies that rose to prominence in Cleveland during the second half of the twentieth century reveals that many of their entrepreneurial founders received their seed money from George Herzog.

Finalizing the Deal

By the end of the week the Central National Bank had agreed to match the offer from Union Commerce. If Dale and I could come up with $1.25 million in equity, it would loan us the rest. Now I had to go back to George Herzog and tell him what had happened. I felt obligated to Central because it had first brought me Automatic Sprinkler, but it was George's enthusiasm for the deal that had given us the confidence to ask Central National for the funds. George assured me we had done the right thing, wished us well, and urged us to keep in touch. Indeed, Union Commerce would ultimately play a crucial role in Automatic Sprinkler's growth, and George's counsel as a board member from 1965 to 1976 would be invaluable.

Dale and I still had to raise more than $1 million, which may as well have been $1 billion to me. My life savings amounted to $27,000. I did find one investor on my own, however. When I asked my neighbor, Jack Doerge, president of the Cleveland brokerage firm, Saunders, Stiver & Company, if he'd be interested in making a $150,000 investment, he overruled his financial advisor and said yes on the spot. He was pretty much going on faith in me, something I never forgot. Jack kept $75,000 for himself and laid off the rest to a friend, Harper Sibley in Rochester, New York. They were rewarded for their confidence in us when, a few years after we went public, they were able to sell their shares for many times their initial investment

Neither Doerge's $150,000 nor my $27,000 made much of a dent in what we still needed. The clock was ticking, and with seven working days left in 1963 Dale realized that there was no way we were going to be able to syndicate more than $1 million in the time that remained. It was then that Dale set up a breakfast meeting with the three principals of Laird and Company—George Weymouth, Martin Fenton, and E. Carroll Stollenwerck. But where was Dale? My entire future was on the line and he was a no-show.

There was no use waiting any longer. Dale was simply not going to show. I took a deep breath and reminded myself of Dale's assurances that these three men could be trusted to listen with open minds, and that they were accustomed to making quick evaluations of people and proposals. I told myself to put aside all extraneous thoughts. I needed to explain to them clearly and concisely exactly what I had in mind. From the age of sixteen I had been dreaming of building a diversified, multi-divisional company and now, at the ripe old age of thirty-nine, I felt that all that stood in my way was the approval of these three men.

I began by telling them a little about myself. I described my experiences at the consulting firm, Booz Allen Hamilton, and about how I was always struck by the fact that a company's profits could rise quickly and dramatically as soon as straightforward cost reduction techniques were implemented. Time after time I had demonstrated to company presidents and plant personnel how costs could be reduced and therefore profits increased, not only for one year, but continually, year after year. I briefly told them about my plans for building a diversified but coordinated corporation through acquisitions. I laid out the financial information concerning Automatic Sprinkler, and assured them that the first and most important task would be to increase its profitability. I explained that as a consultant, and more recently as a group vice president at A.O. Smith, I had helped turn around companies in far worse shape than Automatic, and that I had seen almost every operating problem imaginable. I told the three men that Dale and I already had approval from Cleveland's Central National Bank for a loan of $4.4 million. From Laird and Company I needed a commitment for most of the $1.4 million we still needed. Finally I divulged the most vital piece of information. We needed their money almost immediately, because the sellers insisted that the deal be concluded by December 31 when their $1.7 million tax loss carry forward would expire.

The Laird executives listened politely and asked probing questions. But when we said our goodbyes they were noncommittal, telling me only that they would discuss it with Dale when they saw him.

I flew back to Cleveland, where at 8:30 that evening Dale finally reached me by phone. He apologized for missing the meeting. He had run out of gas on the Merritt Parkway. The good news was that he had spoken with his colleagues at Laird and they were prepared to offer us an $850,000 swing loan, which Dale had promised to lay off by the following March. Just as George Herzog, Jack Doerge, and others had based their enthusiasm for the Automatic Sprinkler deal on their faith in me rather than on any extensive evaluation of Automatic Sprinkler, the principals of Laird and Company, particularly E. Carroll Stollenwerck, backed the deal largely because of their confidence in Dale Coenen.

With the $850,000 commitment from Laird, we now had a week to raise the final $550,000. On Monday, December 23, Dale arranged for us to meet with Hans Ulrich Rinderknecht, president of the Cosmos Bank in Zurich, who happened to be in New York for a few days. Rinderknecht promised us an answer as soon as he returned to Switzerland.

These were frantic days. Dale and I crisscrossed between Cleveland and New York, feverishly trying to put together the money package. At the same time, our lawyers were busy preparing the paperwork so that as soon as the money was raised we could close the deal quickly, before the end of the year.

Finally, on Christmas Day, Dale reached Rinderknecht as he was stepping into the bathtub in his hotel room in Paris. "I need $400,000," Dale told him.

"Okay," Rinderknecht shouted through a poor transatlantic connection.

Dale's call to tell me the news was the best Christmas present I ever received.

I wasn't the only one who took a risk during those closing days of 1963. Just as I would soon be fortunate to assemble a small group of young businessmen to help me build a large corporation, the initial purchase of Automatic Sprinkler would never have been possible without the help of men like Morrie Hartman, George Herzog, Dale Coenen, Jack Doerge, and Uli Rinderknecht. At the time they had no way of knowing if the financial risks they took would pay off.

I was so focused on helping Dale put together the financing that I didn't even visit the plant until after the sale had been finalized. When I walked into the Automatic Sprinkler offices in Youngstown for the first time on that second day of January, 1964, Jack Coakley was waiting for me. "You must be the dumbest man in America," he told me.

"No, I'm the second dumbest," I said. "You sold it."

CHAPTER TWO

Improve the First Building Block

ON THE MORNING OF JANUARY 2, 1964 I used the copier machine as a lectern to address the Automatic Sprinkler employees in Youngstown. Overnight, everything had changed for them. Suddenly their cozy family company was owned and operated by strangers from out of town. They were concerned about the future of their company and their jobs.

I told them that while I was now CEO and chairman, Jack Coakley would remain as president and John Power would continue to run the company as vice president. While I assured them there would be no immediate wholesale changes in personnel, I made no secret that I expected Automatic Sprinkler to be only the first of many acquisitions; that it would serve as the foundation for a multi-divisional company which I hoped would reach $100 million in sales during the next few years and eventually rise to $1 billion. I wanted them to feel they were a crucial part of something important; that they were being given the opportunity to participate in the beginnings of a company that could grow into a large Ohio corporation. I told them I needed their help, that our success depended largely on their belief that together we could accomplish great things.

I wasn't just whistling in the wind. Automatic's experienced workforce was its most valuable asset. Men like Clyde Wood, a nationally known authority on the hydraulic design of sprinklers, had been with Automatic since 1915, and Harry Rider, responsible for the "Rate of Rise" sprinkler system,[6] had joined the company four years later. They and others like them were considered giants in the field.

While the change in ownership certainly made some employees apprehensive, I think for others, particularly the younger people with no Coakley family connection, it was also a time of excitement and expectation. Many of them used it as an opportunity, and some would soon rise to management positions in the much larger public corporation they would help build.

> Profit improvement through cost reduction may not be as flashy or as dramatic as a large increase in sales, but it is much more beneficial to a company's bottom line.

Cost Reduction = Profit Improvement

My goal during the first few months of 1964 was not to increase sales, at least not immediately. Increasing sales is expensive, and often profits take a short term hit. My intention was to increase profits so we would have the cash and the credibility to expand the company through acquisitions and support internal growth.

One decision that had an immediate positive impact on our bottom line was our closing of Automatic Sprinkler's piping subsidiary. That lowered sales by $3 million, but eliminated a losing "profit" center which was absorbing an inordinate share of our working capital.

But there was really only one way I knew to improve profits year in and year out, and that was to make fundamental changes to eliminate waste and improve efficiencies. For years I had been insisting to clients that a comprehensive cost reduction program could take ten percent of total costs out of any company each year

6 In 1943 the Hercules Powder Company was manufacturing a particularly flammable gun powder and asked Automatic for a sprinkler system that would extinguish a fire or explosion before the flames had a chance to spread. Harry Rider developed a system in which "rate of rise" devices were suspended a few inches above the flammable material. When ignited, the valves instantly released showers of water. Rider's ingenuity enabled rocket fuel powder to be produced safely for the remainder of the war.

for three consecutive years. Now I set out with relish to prove it at my own company.

The terms "cost reduction" and "profit improvement" can be used interchangeably. If profit improvement is the glass of water half full, cost reduction is the glass of water half empty. But whatever you call it, there is no more effective way to increase profits. Profit improvement through cost reduction may not be as flashy or as dramatic as, say, a large increase in sales, but it is much more beneficial to a company's bottom line. While a thirty percent increase in a company's sales might be more likely to make the front pages, a ten percent reduction in costs has a much more favorable impact on the company's profits, cash flow, working capital, and competitive position. It can also be used to reduce debt.

The Program

The cost reduction program I developed while at Booz Allen and A.O. Smith and implemented at Automatic Sprinkler and at every subsequent acquisition is just as effective and relevant today as it was fifty years ago. It can be divided into three parts:

- *Part One:* An initial thirty-day program, highlighted by organizational and ratio analyses
- *Part Two:* Setting cost reduction priorities
- *Part Three:* In depth probes, like ABC inventory control, product redesign, accurate sales forecasting, setting standards, and consolidating plants and equipment.

At Automatic Sprinkler, we began implementing parts one and two immediately, starting with an organizational analysis to gauge whether management responsibilities were being managed efficiently. Even a cursory look at a company's organizational chart can indicate whether its span of control is appropriate. Ideally, executives should supervise no less than seven and no more than ten employees, and those responsible for the departments that most affect profits should report directly to the head of the company.

Another step that can be taken immediately is to prioritize your efforts, focusing first on those areas where the company is spending most of its money. As in virtually every manufacturing operation, Automatic Sprinkler spent more on purchasing material than any other single item. My first step, therefore, was to take a look at its purchasing expenditures for December 1963, singling out the ten largest items for particular scrutiny. As usual, the exercise revealed all kinds of unnecessary expenses. At the plant in Indiana we were paying someone to store our pipe so it wouldn't rust even though we had plenty of capacity to store it ourselves. In Maine, we were paying full price to a mill supply house which was simply buying the pipe and putting our fittings on them. We began assembling the part much more inexpensively ourselves.

We also weren't using competition to our advantage. By opening up the purchasing process, we began to influence prices downward. We were spending far too much, for example, for castings from a supplier that had been doing business with Automatic Sprinkler for decades. To prove my point, I asked two other foundries I had worked with while at Booz Allen to submit bids. Our current supplier agreed to drop its price by twenty percent, but I told our purchasing manager to split the order between the three companies, saving us almost $100,000 that first year. When a qualified vendor is invited to submit a bid and comes in with the lowest price, it should be rewarded with at least some of the business. The present supplier shouldn't be allowed to simply match the new prices.

I also found a way to take thirty percent out of the cost of Automatic Sprinkler's largest single expense item, the steel piping that went into our sprinkler systems. When I joined A.O. Smith my group of companies had been purchasing steel wire from the American Steel and Wire Company. I made a deal with a Japanese supplier to deliver rolls of wire to Milwaukee and pay for their storage. This dropped the price from $150 to $106 per ton, and since we were using several hundred tons a month the savings were considerable. Now I made a similar deal with a Japanese consortium to deliver steel piping to Toledo, and to warehouse it at their expense. U.S. manufacturing companies importing steel from Asia would soon become routine, but in 1965 I think we were one of the first to use this strategy to cut costs.

Another important early step in any cost reduction effort is to foster competition among the purchasing department's suppliers. This has to become part of a company's natural order, which often means a wrenching change in the department's normal way of doing business. So there would be no confusion, beginning at Automatic, and subsequently at every company we purchased, our purchasing policy was prominently displayed for all to see. One important message was that suppliers were welcome to pay a call on our purchasing department at any time, and were not restricted to certain hours or days. Another was that our open door policy included encouraging suppliers to make creative suggestions of their own on how we might reduce costs or improve quality.

FIGGIE INTERNATIONAL OPEN DOOR POLICY

At a time when it is becoming an increasingly common practice to restrict the days and hours that salesmen may call, we at Figgie International want you to know that you are welcome at any time or on any day that we conduct business. This is our policy.

We look to you for ideas, suggestions, and creative solutions that will enable us to reduce our costs and to offer the highest standards of quality and service to our customers. We don't think these things can or should be limited to particular days or hours.

As a sales-oriented company, we want you to know that our suppliers are always welcome. We appreciate your interest in our needs and we value your assistance and advice. Since quite a few of us in Figgie International's management came up through selling, we recognize that the salesman's job is not an easy one and we don't intend to make it any harder than it is by establishing arbitrary restrictions

We need you and we ask for your help. We know you won't fail us, and if we fail to treat you fairly, please let me know personally. Thank you for coming in.

Sincerely Yours,
Harry E. Figgie, Jr.
Chairman and Chief Executive Officer

> If the cost of materials as a percentage of sales is increasing, your pricing structure is probably not keeping pace with rising costs. A faulty pricing system can give away all your hard-won cost reduction savings.

The Pitfalls of Pricing

Pricing became an important part of our initial cost reduction efforts at Automatic because a faulty pricing system can give away all, or even more, of a company's hard-won savings. Take a simple example of an item that costs $10 to manufacture and is being sold with a conventional markup of sixty-six percent, or in this case, $16.66. Now assume cost reduction techniques cut $1 from the cost of making that item—from $10 to $9. The controller then passes the revised standard cost figure along to the sales manager, who in turn prices the item at $15—its $9 cost multiplied by the sixty-six percent markup. The result is that having saved $1 in production costs, the sales department has given away $1.67 on each unit sold. It not only knocked out the dollar that had been saved through cost reduction, it took away an additional sixty-seven cents of profit. Top management may not even be aware of what has happened until it is too late—until they take a look at the bottom line and can't understand why the substantial savings gained by the countless hours spent implementing a comprehensive cost reduction program did not translate into an increase in profit, and why in some cases profits actually fell as a percentage of sales. Beware of the inflexibility of a standard cost system. At Automatic, and subsequently at every other acquisition, we put in controls to protect the cost reduction savings and make sure they went directly to our bottom line. I'm still doing this today.

The simplest way to determine whether a company's pricing structure is operating efficiently, and that the hard-won savings gained through cost reduction won't be forfeited by a faulty pricing system, is to keep a careful eye on the cost of materials as a percentage of sales. If that percentage begins to increase, the company's pricing structure has probably not kept pace with rising costs. That's just what I found at Automatic Sprinkler, so we immediately implemented an across-the-board two-percent price increase. Don't be afraid to raise prices. And any time your material, labor, and overhead increase, treat that as a signal that somewhere prices may be arbitrarily being reduced—a situation that requires immediate management attention.

REMEMBER THE FOOTBALL

We had an experience at one of our more recognizable divisions, Rawlings Sporting Goods, that became a rallying cry for the entire corporation. Rawlings manufactured a football with a standard cost of $10, which it sold at wholesale for $20. Using our cost reduction techniques, we reduced costs to $9 per football, which Rawlings proceeded to sell for $18. The division was giving away $2 for every dollar we had saved! At every subsequent cost reduction effort at Rawlings and elsewhere our rallying cry became, "Remember the football!"

No More Santa Claus

Another of Automatic Sprinkler's roadblocks to greater profitability was its sales compensation system. At the time, its commission agreements were based on volume, which guaranteed salesmen a commission regardless of profit and loss to the company. If a salesman sold a $100,000 installation, he received a percentage of that $100,000. The problem was that the system offered no incentive for the salesman to concern himself with the contract's profitability. In fact, it was actually to his advantage to lower his bid in order to make a sale, since his commission was tied to the sale price and not whether the project ultimately turned a profit.

I knew we had to scrap this arrangement. I wanted to foster a feeling that we were all in this together. If the overall corporation was doing well, employees at every level would be compensated accordingly. The reverse was also true. Employees should not expect raises or bonuses, or even job security, if their company was losing money.

I wanted to put into place a standardized system that would shift our emphasis from volume to profits, even if it meant shaking things up for longtime employees. With the help of Booz Allen, we developed a new compensation plan based on the ultimate profitability of each sprinkler installation sold rather than the size of the project. The new formula provided that salesmen receive half their commission up front, based on estimated profit, and the balance after the job was completed, computed on actual profit. Suddenly it was to their advantage to monitor a job to make certain overages or additional requests by the client not in the original contract did not adversely affect the job's profitability.

Another important change was to make certain that everyone involved in a sprinkler installation, not just the salesmen, was focused on its overall profitability. Under the old system, salesmen would write an order, an engineer would design it, and a project director would have the responsibility to carry it to completion in such a way that the company made money. Under our new plan, everyone, not only the project director, had the responsibility, and more importantly, the incentive, to hold down costs. The income of everyone involved was based on the project's ultimate profitability. This encouraged salesmen to go after more profitable types of work and for everyone involved in a job to stay interested in it being completed efficiently. For the first time, each sprinkler installation became its own individual profit center. No longer could salespeople and district managers make a lot of money on projects on which the company didn't make a dime.

We also implemented standard contracts to replace the flimsy one-page letters of agreement that often said little more than that for "x" amount of dollars Automatic Sprinkler would guarantee installation of a sprinkler system that the local fire marshal would approve. We introduced uniformity in how salesmen were compensated in various parts of the country. When we first took over Automatic, in one region of the country the district sales manager was keeping the commissions for himself, while the manager in another region was distributing it to his salesman. The result was that in some district offices we were employing poorly-paid salesmen working under a well-paid district manager, while in others a poorly-paid district manager supervised well-paid salesmen.

There was no more Santa Claus. Now everyone's bonus, as well as the overall health of Automatic Sprinkler, were interconnected. Not everyone appreciated the attributes of the new compensation system, however. Our purchasing manager retired as soon as we announced the wholesale changes in the way his department would operate. Two sales managers and two of the four regional directors also submitted their resignations. "To hell with modern management," one manager told me. "I liked the old way better."

It was pretty scary when our sales force began to walk, but I knew this was something we had to do. I was convinced that the new compensation system was fair, and that Automatic Sprinkler's very existence depended on its success. We had to make everyone at Automatic work for the overall good of the company and not just themselves.

I knew we had our work cut out for us if we hoped to keep our remaining sales force intact. We couldn't expect our salesmen to immediately go along with the changes. We were going to have to prove to them that their well being and the company's well being were one and the same.

Our biggest problem was the sales force's suspicion that the new incentive program was simply a smoke screen to transfer money out of their pockets and into company coffers. This simply wasn't true, but we had to prove it to them.

Dan Carroll, who I knew from my Booz Allen days, had helped me create the new compensation system. Now I engaged him to crisscross the country in an effort to sell our national sales network on its benefits—to both them and the company. At first he took along Jack Coakley because I thought his support would symbolically be important. But Dan came to the conclusion that while the sales force liked Jack, his presence only provoked confusion because it signaled that the old guard and the old way of doing things were still relevant. I agreed that Dan could begin making the rounds alone.

Our salesmen were extremely suspicious of us. They didn't like having to make complicated calculations in order to determine their income, and they didn't think they should be held responsible for cost overruns beyond their control. We used simulations to show them what their compensation would have been the previous year under the new system and to compare the two systems during the current year. We began regular sales meetings to review the new plan, and several times during the latter half of 1964 the entire sales force was flown to Ohio at company expense.

We had to be careful because if the sales force walked, our volume would disappear and the company would collapse. Fortunately, most of our salesmen stuck with us, and once the new formula showed positive results for them and the company, the crisis passed. In fact, with very little alterations, the same compensation philosophy was instituted at other new acquisitions until about one-third of the public company's salaried employees were on some form of incentive compensation.

Pensions

While my primary concern during this first year was to reduce costs, in a few areas we increased them. The company's pension fund, for example, which was close to being bankrupt, was entirely revamped, and the level of benefits in group insurance and health programs were raised. The salaried pension plan we acquired in 1964 had about $330,000 in assets and $3.5 million in unfunded liabilities. The most any employee could receive upon retirement was $122.50 per month, based on thirty-five years of service. We began a program to reduce the pension's unfunded liabilities, while simultaneously substantially boosting benefits. This began a commitment, strengthened once we went public, to make constant improvements in the pension programs at the companies we purchased during the next two decades. It included a strong surviving spouse pension plan that extended to dependent children until they reached the age of twenty-one, or twenty five if they were full-time students. My interest in this area no doubt had something to do with my memory of my father who, only by purchasing life insurance policies shortly before he died, had saved my mother, sister and me from serious financial hardship.

Advertising

Another area where I felt it was necessary to increase spending was our advertising budget. In early 1964 we made a decision to solidify our position as one of the top sprinkler firms in the country by launching a national advertising campaign. In magazines like *Fortune* and *Business Week* we warned about "the high cost of burning":

> The sooner your Automatic Sprinkler fire protection contract is signed, the sooner your business is protected against a devastating fire and the sooner your insurance premium savings go into effect. Don't play with fire. Call us yesterday.

Another ad showed an executive standing at a burned-out building with the caption, "The fire's out and he's out of business."

In our advertising, as well as in our own promotional literature, we pioneered the concept that the cost of installing a sprinkler system could quickly be recouped by the resulting reductions in insurance premiums. We spelled out detailed costs versus savings comparisons, and publicized studies by the American Insurance Association showing that fifty percent of all businesses suffering major fires never start up again, and an additional twenty percent fail within three years.

We also weren't shy about piggybacking on current events. Two weeks after the McCormick Place exhibition hall in Chicago burned down we ran an ad in the *Wall Street Journal* announcing that an Automatic Sprinkler system could have controlled the fire and significantly reduced the $150 million loss. Another ad portrayed a company's grave site, with the text stating that its demise could have been avoided had an Automatic Sprinkler system been installed. To Nancy's consternation, in searching for a non-libelous name to put on the headstone, the advertising agency settled on the "Figgie Tool and Die Works."

Automatic Sprinkler also initiated more active demonstrations of the value of its products. We regularly held two-day seminars at our fire test yard in Youngstown, where we demonstrated the effectiveness of sprinkler systems to corporate and insurance executives and to government engineers involved in the construction of public buildings.

Hire the Hungry

I was fortunate to have a young (average age forty-two), enthusiastic board of directors committed to helping me make my growth plans succeed. Aside from myself (forty) and fifty-two year old John Power, the board consisted mostly of the young men who had helped Dale and me put together the financial package to purchase Automatic Sprinkler, including Jack Doerge, John Gelbach, and Harper Sibley. I relied on Dale and these men to speak about Automatic at every opportunity. The many businesses with which they came into contact—their own companies, other corporations they were affiliated with or on whose boards they served, and even the private clubs to which they belonged—were all prime candidates for the construction of new sprinkler systems. That first year about thirty percent of our new business prospects could be traced to contacts originated by the seven board members besides myself.

And I would need all the help I could get. In late March, less than three months after taking over Automatic Sprinkler, I woke up in the middle of the night with a temperature of 106° and with a pain in my stomach so severe I could barely rise up in bed. In the morning, my wife, Nancy, drove me to the doctor, who was baffled by my symptoms. A friend of mine, who had been a doctor with the 101st Airborne, was nice enough to stop by my house. He diagnosed me with pancreatitis and gave me a massive dose of penicillin and an ice collar to reduce the fever. It turned out I had a duodenal ulcer that had inflamed the pancreas. It took me eleven months to fully recover.

Fortunately, only weeks before I fell ill I had hired as second in command someone I knew I could trust, someone I knew understood what I was trying to do with Automatic Sprinkler. I had met Jim Gilligan in the 1950s when we both were employed by Booz Allen. We had worked closely together on a variety of consulting projects, and had spent many long nights away from home in small

Midwestern towns talking about the concepts on which successful companies were built. We had kept in touch when Jim moved to California to take a job with U.S. Industries, and later when he moved to the Northern Natural Gas Company in Omaha, as director of cost control and later as manager of corporate planning.

Gilligan, a graduate of the Wharton School of Finance, was one of the very early computer experts in the corporate world. Back in January 1964, as soon as he learned of my acquisition of Automatic Sprinkler, he took the data I gave him over the phone and had his team of computer specialists at Northern Natural Gas develop a program to test the cost reduction and return on investment estimates that Dale and I had calculated on paper. We had optimistically estimated a return on investment of thirty-five percent, but Jim's computer analysis predicted fifty-one percent. That only added to my confidence that I could make something of the small sprinkler company.

In February I hired Jim as vice president of finance, with an initial charge to introduce new computer techniques into Automatic's antiquated billing and design practices. Under the old regime, calculating the cost and implementation of a single sprinkler system typically took fifty-five man hours. With the help of a computer specialist he brought with him from Northern Gas, Gilligan supervised the creation of a program that spun out twenty different design concepts in less than a half hour, starting with the least expensive with a minimum of frills and ending with the most elaborate and most expensive. At the time, I think we were the only company in the sprinkler field that could design a sprinkler system and do all the hydraulic calculations on a computer.

With me ill and immobilized, Gilligan became my eyes and ears. Propped up in bed, I spoke with him by telephone constantly and we met at my house each weekend. I was pretty much running the company from my bedroom, although I did make every board meeting. I would pop a handful of aspirin to knock my fever down, go to the director's meeting, and return home to collapse.

These were tenuous times. All the changes we were implementing actually increased our short term expenses, and profits were still being squeezed by the old compensation system and the one-time expense of closing down Automatic's piping subsidiary. At one point Jim called me on my sick bed to ask, "Do I put in the flexible variable budget or do I call in the banks?" I told him I liked the sound of the flexible variable budget. We were confident we had already implemented enough cost reduction savings to improve profits. Indeed, by year's end we had reduced total operating costs by $1.6 million, much of it from the purchasing area. As a result, while sales had risen just eleven percent, from $22.7 million to $25.2 million, pretax profits had more than tripled, from $334,000 to $1,116,000.

We used the cash to accelerate our debt payment, liquidating $1.5 million of the bank's notes within the first two years. "Don't worry," I assured the banks. "We'll be back for more." Now that we had lowered our interest costs, we could use future borrowings for acquisitions.

CHAPTER THREE

Build Through Acquisitions

> When old line firms like General Electric diversify they're called diversified companies. As the new kids on the block, we were called *conglomerates*.

WITHIN TWELVE MONTHS WE HAD succeeded in completing the first step of building a large diversified company. By early 1965 sales and profits had exceeded even the optimistic projections of Gilligan's computers. The value of construction in process at year end was at a record level, representing a backlog double that of 1963.

My health had finally improved, and we were primed to begin an acquisition strategy that would grow us into a much larger company. Not only had Automatic Sprinkler been made profitable, once the new sales compensation system and the other major cost reductions were incorporated into routine corporate policy, Jim Gilligan and I were free to concentrate on the expansion of the company as a whole rather than on the Automatic Sprinkler division in particular. Sprinkler was operating efficiently on its own with the very competent John Power still at the helm.

Conglomerate or Not

As Dale Coenen, Jim Gilligan, and I set our sights on developing a diversified company through acquisitions, we had no idea other businessmen in other parts of the country had similar plans. I had never heard of terms like leveraged buyouts or conglomerate mergers. A few years later these terms would be plastered on business pages across the country. Nor was I aware that men like Royal Little (Textron), James Ling (LTV Corporation), Tex Thorton (Litton Industries), Harold Geneen (ITT), and Charles Bludhorn (Gulf & Western) were embarked on a similar strategy of building what the press dubbed, conglomerates.

Perhaps the one thing all of us had in common[8] was that none of us much liked the term, conglomerate. As someone trained in metallurgy, I was well aware of the geological definition of the word—"an amorphous mass of rocks held together by a common matrix." The typical dictionary definition of conglomeration was no better—"a mixed collection, a hodgepodge." No wonder we disliked the label, derived from the Latin words "com" meaning together and "glomus" meaning "wax." I wasn't putting together an amorphous mass of companies with no relationship between divisions. I think conglomerate was just a lazy way for the media to label a new kind of large diversified company that they didn't really understand. It seemed to me that when old line companies like General Electric diversified they were called "diversified companies," while as the new kids on the block, we were called conglomerates. At any rate, conglomerate was the name we were all stuck with.

That so many of us began building conglomerates simultaneously wasn't exactly a coincidence, since antitrust legislation had largely put the breaks on large acquisitions within the same industry. Until the 1950s, corporations intent on building themselves by acquiring other companies generally did so through concentration and specialization. Companies like Standard Oil of New Jersey and American Tobacco perfected the art of the vertical takeover, by which they acquired suppliers and distributors for products they manufactured. Others used the horizontal merger to increase market

8 There was something else we had in common. A friend of mine once pointed out to me the startling coincidence that so many of us who built diversified companies in the 1960s grew up without a father. Royal Little, who transformed Textron Inc. into what was probably the first of the modern conglomerates, lost his father at the age of four. Tex Thorton, who turned the $3 million Litton Industries into a multi-billion dollar diversified company, as well as Harold Geneen of ITT, also grew up without fathers. And Charles Bludhorn, the force behind Gulf & Western, left home when he was 11 and by 16 was living alone in New York City, a refugee from Nazi Europe.

share. General Motors became big by acquiring Buick, Oldsmobile, and Pontiac. Rarely was there any mystery about what kind of business any particular corporation was in. Names like American Tobacco, Dow Chemical, General Foods, General Motors, and United States Steel needed no explanation.

By the 1960s, however, legislation strengthening the 1890 Sherman Antitrust Act discouraged the largest of these kinds of vertical and horizontal mergers. That's when a handful of us began to use a new kind of growth strategy in which the companies we acquired were not necessarily in our current line of business. This kind of "circular" takeover had no anti-competitive effect on the economy, so did not conflict with antitrust laws.

> It's better to walk on six legs than on one or two.

Nucleus Theory

I wasn't thinking about the difference between circular and vertical takeovers when I started building Automatic Sprinkler through acquisitions. I had my own plan for what I wanted to do, which I called the nucleus theory of growth. It's based on the idea that it is best to acquire companies in industries experiencing better than average growth, then build within those industries by acquiring related companies. The first acquisition within each growth industry is called the nucleus. Additional companies in that industry are then added in order to complement and expand the nucleus.

The nucleus theory is essentially the selection, acquisition and internal development of companies within major industries and with complementary product lines. There's no reason it couldn't be used today to build a diversified corporation from scratch just as it was 40-plus years ago.

NUCLEUS THEORY

1. Identify an industry with growth potential.
2. Acquire a company within that industry to serve as a nucleus, or flagship operation.
3. Implement a three-part program within each nucleus of cost reduction, sales and market expansion, and research and development.
4. Acquire additional companies within the selected nucleus industry and implement the same three-step program at each new operation.

Growth prospects for each nucleus industry must in some way be quantifiable, either by determining that its products will fill a continuing need in the economy, or that new products of particular benefit can be identified, developed and marketed. Each nucleus should represent an industry dominated by a number of small and medium-size firms rather than one or two giants.

The original nucleus company should also be in a growth field in which foreign competition will not be a dominating factor for the foreseeable future and in which you have some expertise. Automatic Sprinkler fit both those criteria, and had the added benefit in that I knew I wouldn't have to pour a lot of working capital into it. It was more of an installation and sales business than an operation that depended on factories working efficiently and having to be modernized.

Because of inflation, all these numbers have at least doubled, but at the time I wanted each company we acquired as the start of a new nucleus to be doing at least $20 million in sales. I've always believed this to be the critical mass size. Anything below that, you sneeze and you're out of business, or you'll spend your lifetime building the company to $20 million and then you've got very little time left to make it grow. It took me longer to increase sales at my family company, Clark Reliance, from $250,000 to $10 million, than it did to move the public company from $20 million to $1 billion. My consulting experience taught me that small companies have all the problems of large companies, but less money, time and manpower to find the solutions. It's just like Cash McCall said: "Successful companies come in two sizes these days. Small and large. It's the medium-sized ones that have the tough go—too big to be handled with one-man management, not big enough to support a real organization."

From a $20 million start, our goal was to build each nucleus as quickly as possible, mostly through acquisitions, until they reached $100 million in sales. Ideally the companies we acquired would have sales of $20 million, but in our early years this was rarely the case. We could generally afford only smaller, ailing companies which we had to nurse to $20 million before growing the nucleus to $100 million and more. I tried to focus on industries in which a $75–$100 million company would constitute a position of considerable importance.

The nucleus theory gave us flexibility in deciding what kinds of businesses to enter. It provided a central, coordinated theme that we could intelligently explain to the media, security analysts, and the owners and employees of potential acquisitions. It also allowed us to organize the company along product lines, and develop expertise and market share in a handful of growth industries, which we could then use to increase market share. The nucleus theory provides an excellent framework for management, in that related divisions can be managed at the corporate level by a group executive familiar with the overall market, as well as specific product lines. It also allows for a small, highly mobile corporate staff to place responsibility for profit-making decisions at the division level. Each division president has entrepreneurial-like control of his company's fortunes, including profit and growth targets. In this streamlined organization, a division president reports to a group vice president, who in turn reports directly to the president or chairman.

As the company matured, our combination of size and diversification protected us from the fluctuations of any one industry or division, and gave us balance in every kind of financial climate. In a diversified company with six nucleuses, it's difficult to come up with a scenario in which all six businesses would be experiencing a downturn simultaneously. Today, with so much more competition and shorter life cycles, the benefits of diversification are even greater. It's better to walk on six legs than on one or two.

The initial acquisition that creates a new nucleus should be in an industry:

- That has quantifiable growth prospects
- That will not be dominated by international competition for the foreseeable future
- That is not dominated by one or two giants
- In which a $75-100 million company represents a position of considerable importance
- In which you have some experience

Assembling a Team

Jim Gilligan and I knew we would need a lot of help in order to launch the kind of ambitious acquisition program we had in mind. A year after purchasing Automatic Sprinkler our corporate staff still consisted of only the two of us. To start with, we needed someone to organize the increasing influx of mail, phone calls and visitors that had begun to bombard our Youngstown offices—someone to play traffic cop, office manager, switchboard operator, scribe, librarian, and mailman. I tapped my former secretary at A.O. Smith, Mary Cleary, for the job.

Shy and reserved, the red haired, quick-to-blush Mary Cleary was first generation Irish. Her soft, quavering voice was a stranger to four-letter words, which made her somewhat unique in the early rough and tumble days of Automatic Sprinkler's rapid growth. Len Barbee, soon to be hired as director of manufacturing, gave her the nickname, "Mother Mary." She was my secretary for more than thirty years, but never stopped calling me "Mr. Figgie."

Gilligan and I had been working primarily out of our homes in Cleveland. In May, just before Mary came aboard, we rented three small rooms in the CEI Building, a downtown office tower anchoring one corner of Cleveland's Public Square. I also hired two men who would be instrumental in helping us implement our acquisition program. Short, squat Leonard Barbee, "The Greek," to some of his friends, had been working on the factory floor since leaving school after the fourth grade to help support his family. He started at A.O. Smith in 1946 as an assembly man in a water heater division in Kankakee, Illinois for $32 a week and worked his way up to plant manager at one of the companies in my A.O. Smith industrial group. Barbee was the ultimate "operator." Introduced to a new piece of machinery, he liked to take it apart and put it together again in an effort to make it more efficient, or at least to learn how it worked in preparation for when it broke down. He was sure of himself and argumentative; a straight shooter and a straight talker.

Barbee never tolerated orders from his superiors that he felt were unwarranted, a trait that kept him moving around in the vast, conservative A.O. Smith organization. That gained him broad experience on the manufacturing floor within various industries. We got to know each other when he was general superintendent of A. O. Smith's Glascote division, a manufacturer of glass-lined chemical reactors. Glascote was the biggest money loser in my group, so I spent a lot of time there, particularly on weekends. Walking the plant, trying to figure out what to do to turn Glascote around, I'd pepper Barbee with questions. He always had some kind of answer, even if it went against the party line.

Also in May we hired Dameron Davis as director of Industrial Relations. "If you come with us, bring your track shoes," warned Gilligan, who had worked with him at U.S. Industries. Davis and Len Barbee were hired on the same day, at the same hour, of the same year. But Barbee was hired in the Midwest and Davis on the west coast, so Barbee had seniority, something he never hesitated to point out to Davis during the next two decades.

Dameron was just the right tough, experienced negotiator we, as new kids on the block, needed. Jim Gilligan like to say that Dameron "never got caught at the far end of a square room with only one door." One time he and Barbee were negotiating at Kersey Manufacturing and the negotiations had come to an impasse. The union representative told them they wanted to caucus. "You want to caucus or cactus?" Davis asked. "What's the difference?" wondered the union rep. "Well," said Davis, "on a cactus the pricks are on the outside." The union, of course, insisted that Davis and Barbee go outside.

Although we employed a local firm as our outside legal counsel, the one other person I thought we needed was an in-house attorney who could make sense of the countless laws and regulations with which mergers and acquisitions had to comply. In 1965 Lou Harthun was thirty years old. He had a two year old son and another child on the way. His family and his wife's family all lived within two hundred miles of their recently purchased home in a comfortable suburb west of Chicago. His future was secure with one of the top law firms in Illinois. Then I came along and offered him a $1500 cut in salary, with no guarantees that the company would survive the year. But I think that when Lou met with Gilligan, Barbee and me, he found our enthusiasm to be contagious. A few months after joining us he told me how struck he was with the difference between his new job and working in private practice. It wasn't so much the physical contrast between his dark paneled, book-lined law office and his off-white cubby-hole in the CEI Building. In private practice an attorney was supposed to maintain a certain degree of professional detachment. You're taught that if you become too embroiled in the work, your effectiveness will suffer. But Lou told me the opposite was true once he joined Automatic. Suddenly it wasn't what he was doing for them, the clients. There was only us, and we were either going to win or lose depending on how well each of us performed. That feeling energized all of us.

> It was a great lesson. In the future I always carefully watched my debt-to-equity ratio.

Going Public

In addition to assembling a team, we had another important step to take before embarking on our acquisition campaign in earnest. It was always the intention of Dale and me to bring Automatic Sprinkler public. Not only would stock be another way to pay for acquisitions, but we had promised our early investors that they would have the opportunity to sell their stock in a public market and be rewarded for the risk they had taken in bankrolling the original purchase of Automatic Sprinkler.

The Coakleys, however, put up a roadblock by insisting that their warrants be honored before the company was brought public. We tried to convince them to stick with us, but we were forced to buy back their preferred shares at par, retire their warrants for $920,000, and come up with another $1.2 million to retire their debt.

I suppose I can't really blame the Coakleys for wanting to see their cash prior to the company going public. There was no guarantee their warrants would ever be worth more than they were at that moment. But others stuck with us and were rewarded for their confidence. Those same warrants for which the Coakleys received less than $1 million would have been worth many times that amount just a year or two later.

Buying out the Coakleys really stretched our balance sheet, but all we could do was hold our breath until we went public. I knew we were in trouble when a Boston Bank executive laughed at me when I came to him with the idea of becoming a public company by acquiring the publicly traded Whitin Machine Company, a Massachusetts manufacturer of textile machinery. I thought it was a brilliant idea because it would have avoided the trouble of an initial public offering of our own. But the banker pointed out that after buying out the Coakleys, we were leveraged at a six-to-one debt-to-equity ratio, with more than $12 million of ninety-day loans and only slightly more than $2 million in equity. "If you hiccup before you go public you won't be able to cover your debt and you'll be out of business," he warned. I told him I had no intention of hiccupping. But it was a great lesson. In the future I always carefully watched our debt-to-equity ratio.

Dale and I knew that the solution was to go public, but no brokerage firm was going to agree to that until we increased our equity. Again I turned to George Herzog, president of the Union Commerce Bank, who issued for us what became known as the "Herzog Preferred." In three hours he put away $1 million by taking $200,000 for himself and laying off the rest to four friends, including Howard Metzenbaum, soon to be elected to the United States Senate from Ohio. In return, these investors got the option to convert their investment into shares of stock in the new company.

On November 17, 1965 Laird and Company of New York and Saunders, Stiver & Company of Cleveland brought Automatic Sprinkler onto the Over the Counter Market with a public offering of 242,210 shares. 110,000 shares were sold by Automatic Sprinkler, and 132,210 by our group of early investors.

Dale had already fulfilled his commitment to his associates at Laird and Company by laying off the $850,000 that they had committed in December 1963. Bessemer Securities had taken most of it, and after we went public they ended up as our largest single shareholder, with twenty-one percent of the outstanding shares. Uli Rinderknecht's Cosmos Bank owned slightly more than ten percent, and my family and I owned about fifteen percent.

The successful public offering really liberated us. We used the cash, along with the money raised from the Herzog Preferred, to reduce debt, lowering our debt-to-equity ratio to a much more manageable level of one to one. It also allowed us to enter 1966 with the two most important resources necessary to make additional acquisitions—stock, combined with a decent debt-to-equity ratio. It didn't hurt that our stock price almost immediately jumped from its initial price of $19.50 per share to $28. By September it had risen to more than $56 a share and we tripled the number of shares outstanding, paving the way for a five to two stock split. By the end of the year, sales were up to more than $90 million, double what they had been in 1965 and about four times the size of the 1964 company before our acquisition program began. Net income and earnings per share also doubled.

There were several accounting rules that benefited diversified companies, and we quickly learned their magic:

- When one company acquires another with a lower price/earnings ratio, the combination of the two companies creates a price/earnings ratio greater than either one had prior to the acquisition.

- Using pooled results, the acquiring company is allowed to pretend it owned the acquired company for the entire year, artificially boosting earnings per share.

But pooled figures serve no useful function as a yardstick for measuring performance. The price you offer for a company should be based on your assessment of its potential and its value to your own operation. Eventually every acquiring company has to consolidate what it has purchased and prove that it can make an improved profit.

We didn't consider ourselves conglomerateurs. We were operators, intent on using the nucleus theory and our profit improvement expertise to build a successful diversified company.

Using the Rules

A high stock price was certainly one important ingredient of a successful acquisition program, but there were others, and we immersed ourselves in the various ways the tax code and accounting regulations could be put to our advantage. For example, most of our early acquisitions were family companies in which estate planning as one of the prime motivations to sell. When an entrepreneur, after having spent years building his company, suddenly died, his heirs were faced with inheritance tax obligations. Congress only recently rolled back the inheritance tax, scheduling it to be revoked altogether in 2010. Prior to this, however, when a family company constituted the bulk of an owner's estate, it would often have to be sold just to pay the taxes. As a result, many owners of private companies needed liquidity. If they sold their company for stock while they were still alive, there was usually no immediate income tax liability. Then when the time came, the estate would be liquid enough to fund the estate taxes. The inclusion of a publicly traded stock also generally made the estate valuation more precise.

There were several other important accounting rules that benefited diversified companies. One technique was the "pooling of interest" method for accounting for acquisitions, which boosted both reported sales volume and earnings per share. Under the traditional "purchase method" of accounting, one company simply buys another for cash or other negotiable paper. The sale price of most companies is usually in excess of book value. The difference between the book value and the price actually paid, called the "premium," is either allocated to assets or, more frequently, to "intangibles," often euphemistically referred to as "goodwill."

Not only does goodwill imply that you paid too much for the company, but it is usually not tax-deductible. This means that the annual amortization of the goodwill translated into a direct pretax charge to the company's published income statement. Goodwill, therefore, has a negative impact on profits, as well as on earnings per share, Wall Street's favorite tool for determining the price of a company's stock.

Instead, many diversified companies used the pooling of interest method to account for acquisitions. In this case, a target company is acquired for stock rather than cash, and the acquiring company is permitted to assume, for the purposes of reporting earnings, that it has always owned the company it has just purchased. Not only can the sale be structured in such a way that the stock received is not immediately taxable to the former owners, there is also no

The fire's out and he's out... of business

It could happen faster than you think. Over 50% of all businesses struck by major fires never reopen their doors. Another 20% fail within three years. Fire insurance softens the blow but it can't replace key employees who take other jobs, customers who find new suppliers or equipment, drawings and tooling which may take years to duplicate. Delivery time on a milling machine, for example, is 13 months. ▪ Major fire loss can be eliminated or drastically reduced by an "Automatic" Sprinkler Corporation fire protection system. Whether you lease or buy, your savings on fire insurance premiums will pay for the system in a few years. Talk it over with your nearby "Automatic" representative. He's listed in the Yellow Pages. Your security is our only business.

FORTUNE July 1965 7

Fortune, July 1965

"Automatic" Sprinkler systems put out fires almost anywhere.

In peanut factories and posh hotels.

In NASA missiles and suburban schools.

In cotton warehouses and old folks homes.

Wherever valuable people are gathered, wherever valuable things are stored, an "Automatic" Sprinkler System belongs.

Let us give you two hard-headed business reasons why you should buy what we're selling today:

1. You can't afford a fire. 50% of the businesses that burn down shut down immediately. Another 20% fold up within three years. Why? Because the cost of rebuilding a modern structure to conform with modern building codes often exceeds the insurance coverage on the old building. And because during the reconstruction period, employees find new jobs, customers find new suppliers, and you get lost in the shuffle.

2. You can afford "Automatic" Sprinkler protection. If you buy an "Automatic" Sprinkler system, you'll be able to pay for it out of reduced fire insurance premiums in a comparatively short period of time. After that, insurance savings continue to reduce your operating expenses and improve profits. The protection remains. If you'd rather lease than buy, you can get your "Automatic" Sprinkler protection with no capital outlay. Reduced fire insurance premiums not only cover the cost of the lease, but also add pre-tax profits.

Ask your insurance agent to quote you his low preferred risk, FIA, or Factory Mutual rates for sprinklered buildings.

Ask us to show you how we can meet your total fire protection needs. Environmental or operational. Simple or sophisticated. Normal or special hazards.

You're paying protection money anyhow.

So why not protect yourself?

See how an "Automatic" Sprinkler System can cut your fire insurance premiums up to 90%.

PROPERTY	Annual Premium Before Sprinklers	Annual Premium After Sprinklers	Annual Lease Payment	Extra Dollars to Profit During Lease	Extra Dollars to Profit After Lease
Distributor Warehouse	$ 5,600	$1,650	$2,502	$1,448	$ 3,950
Furniture-Manufacturer	7,100	720	1,485	4,915	6,380
Hotel	21,494	4,700	9,784	7,010	16,794
Metal Fabrication Plant	5,600	1,650	1,704	2,246	3,950

Write for revealing free brochure entitled "The High Cost of Burning."

DON'T PLAY WITH FIRE. CALL US YESTERDAY.

DEPT. F-96 YOUNGSTOWN, OHIO 44501

Meet the growing family of "Automatic" Sprinkler: American LaFrance Division • "Auto-Grip" Division • "Automatic" Process Piping Co., Inc. • Badger Fire Extinguisher Company, Inc. • Fee & Mason Manufacturing Company, Inc. • Kersey Manufacturing Co. • Powhatan Brass & Iron Works • William Stanley Company

220 FORTUNE September 1966

Fortune, September 1966

70% of all businesses that burn down die out.

50% never re-open.

Another 20% shut down within three years.

Pretty frightening percentages for a hard-headed businessman to ignore. But not frightening enough to keep a lot of you from thinking: "It can't happen to me."

It *can* happen to you. Suddenly. Devastatingly. And while you struggle to rebuild, your employees go on to other things. Your customers forget you.

You can't afford a fire.

You certainly *can* afford the fire protection of an "Automatic" Sprinkler system.

Most installations pay for themselves out of reduced fire insurance premiums within a few years. After that, your insurance savings can be used to increase profits or reduce operating expense. The protection remains. (Some companies prefer to lease their sprinkler systems to avoid any capital outlay.

Ask your insurance agent how businesses with "Automatic" Sprinkler systems can qualify for his low preferred risk, FIA or Factory Mutual fire insurance rates.

Ask us how we can meet your total fire protection requirements . . . environmental or operational, simple or sophisticated, normal or special hazards.

Ask.

Insurance Savings with "Automatic" Sprinkler Protection

PROPERTY	Annual Insurance Cost Before Sprinklers	Annual Insurance Cost After Sprinklers	Sprinkler System Cost	Annual Savings	Sprinkler System Amortization
Processing Plant	$6,136.00	$940.00	$24,900.00	$5,196.00	5 years
Warehouse	2,316.00	345.00	4,788.00	1,971.00	2½ years
Manufacturing Plant	5,899.00	468.00	13,950.00	4,792.00	3 years
Printing Plant	1,590.00	357.00	3,500.00	1,233.00	3 years

Write for revealing free brochure entitled "The High Cost of Burning."

DON'T PLAY WITH FIRE. CALL US YESTERDAY.

"Automatic" Sprinkler
CORPORATION OF AMERICA
DEPT F-66 YOUNGSTOWN, OHIO 44501

Meet the growing family of "Automatic" Sprinkler: "Auto-Grip" Division • "Automatic" Process Piping Co., Inc. • Badger Fire Extinguisher Company, Inc. Fee & Mason Manufacturing Company, Inc. • Kersey Manufacturing Company • Powhatan Brass & Iron Works • William Stanley Company

190 FORTUNE *June 1966*

Fortune, June 1966

Fortune, May 1970

A corporation needs an extraordinary growth record before they can ask a question like that.
We think we have one.
We've grown from $25 million in sales (as reported*) to $379 million in five years. On the same basis our net worth grew from $4 million to $94 million; and our total assets grew from $11 million to $237 million. Yet we have the strongest balance sheet in the company's history. And we have $100 million in net working capital right now. Our current assets alone ($171 million) exceed our total liabilities by more than $28 million.
Backing all this up with a large, strong line of credit is a 12-member group of the most respected and progressive bankers in the country.
That means we can continue to grow. It means we've got what it takes to provide any new plants or equipment required . . . to finance continued internal growth . . . to develop and market new products . . . to further our planned acquisition program . . . to carry us through the current tight money situation, or even a recession. For more detailed information about our growing giant, ask your broker or write for a copy of our 1969 annual report. A-T-O Inc., 55 Public Square, Cleveland, Ohio 44113. A $379 million international corporation that's growing. Strong.
ATO
Formerly "Automatic" Sprinkler Corporation of America.
*$179 million restated to include pooled acquisitions.

Wouldn't it be smart for a great company manufacturing fire detection, alarm, and sprinkler systems to get together with a great company manufacturing fire engines, fire extinguishers, and fire department supplies?

AMERICAN LaFRANCE

ELMIRA, N. Y.

They just did.

(American LaFrance is now a member of the growing "Automatic" Sprinkler Corporation family.)

Fortune, June 1966

Fortune, September 1966

Our corporation moves so fast it had its 1970 recession in 1968.

We took a real beating. But what happened to us in 1968 has given us a jump in preparing for the recession that might come in 1970. In the past twelve months we've been busy:

Consolidating our divisions for greater operating efficiency and installing the cost-control programs that others are just now setting up to ease the pressure on corporate profits.

Reducing our debt, materially strengthening our balance sheet, and getting the corporation in good financial position to live with tight money or even ride out a recession.

Teaching modern management techniques that pay off in better performance . . . during good times or bad.

Building the depth and strength of our management team.

In short, we've tightened our belt. So that while others are "adjusting", we'll be moving ahead. Because we've already done a lot of the things that need doing to get a better future return on each sales dollar. And we're going to do more.

A-T-O Inc., Cleveland, Ohio. A $375 million international corporation that's moving. Ahead. Fast.

ATO

Formerly "Automatic" Sprinkler Corporation of America.

Fortune, January 1970

From the 1973 ATO annual report.

allocation of purchase price to goodwill. Instead, profits of the acquired company are combined with those of the acquiring company immediately, boosting reported earnings for the year in which the deal takes place. Even if the transaction is concluded in December, the acquiring company is allowed to assume that it owned the company for the entire year, thus temporarily and artificially boosting earnings per share.

I was always a vocal critic of pooled figures, which serve no useful function as a yardstick for measuring performance. They fail to take into account the long range value of an acquired company in relation to what you paid for it. The price you offer for a company is not based entirely on what it has done in the past, or even on its current performance, but on your assessment of its potential and its value to your own operation. It is impossible to make meaningful performance comparisons by measuring actual earnings against hypothetical pooled results. The real criteria for evaluating performance is the actual earnings increases reported. The pooling method ultimately fell out of favor with Wall Street and the accounting profession stopped using it altogether.

Another result of the pooling of interest method of accounting was that when one company acquired another with a lower price/earnings ratio, the combination of the two companies created a price/earnings ratio greater than either one had prior to the acquisition. Assume Company A has a million shares outstanding, each selling for $20 a share with earnings per share of $1. Company A decides to acquire Company B, which also has a million shares outstanding earning $1 per share. But because Company B is not a growth company, or for some other reason is not a Wall Street favorite, its stock is selling at only $5 a share. Company A acquires 100% of Company's B stock for $7.50 a share, a fortuitous deal for the shareholders of Company B, who receive fifty percent more for their shares than they could have sold them for on the open market. They either end up with $7.5 million in cash, or stock worth the same amount but which is not taxable at the time of the transaction.

If the stock has been swapped, Company A has traded 375,000

of its own shares for all of Company B's million shares. So the acquiring company is capitalized at 1,375,000 shares and has annual sales of $2 million. This works out to earnings per share not of $1 as before the merger, but to $1.45.

One Plus One Equals Three			
	Total Shares	Share Price	Earnings Per Share
Company A	1 million	$20	$1
Company B	1 million	$5	$1
Combined Company	1.375 million		$1.45

Company A buys Company B for $7.50 per share; pays for it with 375,000 shares. Combined company has 1.375 million shares with earnings of $2 million, or earnings per share of $1.45.

Although the new company is immediately no better or worse than the sum of its parts prior to the merger, earnings per share have increased forty-five percent. By acquiring additional companies in precisely this same manner, Company A can continue to boost its earnings per share, which increases its status on Wall Street and often leads to even larger price/earnings ratios, which propel the price of its stock to new highs.

The more cynical observers argued that it was actually to the advantage of conglomerates to acquire poorly-run companies, ones that had low earnings per share. In this case they didn't have to sell more widgets, reduce their overhead, or improve their product in order to create a more successful company. All they had to do was use their high stock price to keep making acquisitions.

Such a numbers game could not continue indefinitely, of course, since there was a fatal flaw in boosting earnings per share without increasing the real value or worth of the combined company. Eventually every acquiring company has to consolidate what it has purchased and prove that it can make an honest profit.

Certainly no one was accusing Automatic Sprinkler of deliberately looking for poorly-run companies so that we could artificially increase earnings per share. Although we often purchased companies that were not profitable in order to place them in an already existing nucleus, we did it because we could afford them and believed we had the expertise to turn them around. We were operators, intent on using the nucleus theory and our profit improvement expertise, rather than more ethereal tax and accounting techniques, to build a successful diversified company.

Have bank approval prior to shaking hands on any deal.

It is important that your experts keep you current concerning tax, accounting, and reporting requirements in effect at the time of your acquisition.

The Nucleus Theory in Action

Now that Automatic Sprinkler was running smoothly and profitably, we began our acquisitions program by looking for companies that would logically fit into our first nucleus, fire protection, and build upon Automatic Sprinkler's existing operations. First we bought two small companies in the portable fire extinguisher business, Badger Metal Products and Safety House, both of which we were able to finance by internally generated funds. Next we paid $2.5 million for Powhatan Brass & Iron Works, again for cash since we had not yet gone public. Powhatan had a product line of more than 3,500 different items, mostly brass fittings for fire sprinkler systems, fire trucks, and other fire fighting equipment.

I felt I should always have bank approval prior to shaking hands on any deal. That way, I could negotiate in good faith, knowing that I could back up any offer I made. I learned this the hard way after a Cleveland bank suddenly reneged on its commitment to loan us $6 million to purchase the American LaFrance fire truck company.

This banker told us that the economy had picked up and that the bank's large clients now had additional working capital requirements. We scrambled for an alternative, and the Bank of Boston agreed to loan us the full amount. As if to prove the old saw that banks only loan money to those who don't need it, the Cleveland bank then reversed course once again and agreed to grant us the loan. But by this time we had made the Bank of Boston our lead bank, even though the decision gave us a black eye with the Cleveland banking community that lasted for decades.

American LaFrance, founded in 1872 by the brothers Asa and Truckson LaFrance, was an important acquisition for us. The companies that made up American LaFrance had pioneered some of the most important fire fighting innovations of the twentieth century, including the first gasoline engine and the first motorized ladder apparatus. In May 1966, with the acquisition of LaFrance (which had sales of just under $15 million), we became the largest integrated fire protection company in the United States, surpassing the industry leader, Grinnell Corporation, in total sales

Another nucleus I had anticipated creating during my Booz Allen years was in the broad field of labor reduction. I thought that companies manufacturing labor saving equipment would be able to exploit the rapid technological advancements that were occurring. Acquisitions like Kersey Manufacturing, a producer of electrical vehicles for the mining industry; Hydraxtor, a manufacturer and marketer of industrial washing machines; and Safway Steel, a leader in construction scaffolding, combined to form this second nucleus, industrial equipment related to labor reduction.

As a public company, we could now use stock to make more substantial acquisitions, and in early 1968 we made our largest purchase yet, the bottling manufacturer, George Meyer, which had had sales of more than $63 million in 1967. Other nucleuses soon followed. With the purchase of the pipe hanger manufacturer, Fee and Mason, we created the fluid controls and hydraulic equipment nucleus. Scott Aviation, a manufacturer of oxygen equipment, and Interstate Engineering, which provided test instrumentation and range tracking systems for submarines, became the centerpieces of our defense nucleus. And the purchase of Rawlings Sporting Goods in November 1967, combined with Safway Steel's portable bleachers and gymnasium seating and Interstate's consumer products division, formed our consumer-recreation products nucleus.

> Be on the lookout for concerns which aren't so blue chip that you can't afford them, but not so sick that they won't be susceptible to profit improvement.
>
> Value companies the same way you do a new piece of equipment, based on how long it will take to pay back the purchase price from earnings.
>
> EBITDA (earnings before interest, taxes, depreciation, and amortization) is for financiers; cash flow and payback are for entrepreneurs.
>
> Before making an offer, find out why a company is for sale.

Searching for Gems

Once we got a reputation as an acquirer, leads and offerings came in from all sorts of sources. During our most prolific acquisition period, from 1965 to 1968, we received suggestions on about 100 companies each month, investigated about half of them on paper, and visited a dozen or so in person. In one 25-day period in 1967 we closed five deals. Some possibilities came literally over the transom, slipped through the mail slot or under the door. Sometimes one of us got an idea after reading the business pages of the *Cleveland Plain Dealer* or *Wall Street Journal*. Others were suggested by members of Automatic Sprinkler's board of directors, particularly Dale Coenen, who, as an investment banker at Laird and Company, was in a position to keep a lookout for companies we might want to purchase. Our division presidents also became a great source of identifying potential companies in their respective areas. Most often, investment bankers, brokers, or other interested parties called with news of a company for sale "too good to pass up."

Sometimes a company would attract our interest because it was in a business that years ago, as a consultant, I had decided had good growth potential. Other times it was because a company fit into a nucleus we had already established, or one which we were interested in starting. Always we were on the lookout for concerns which weren't so blue chip that we couldn't afford them, but not so sick that they wouldn't be susceptible to our program of cost reductions and profit improvements.

Once we identified a company worthy of consideration, we scheduled a face-to-face meeting with its owner and other top management. Barbee would proceed directly to the plant floor, where in his usual peripatetic style, he would walk up and down the aisles inspecting every piece of machinery and method. He would also talk to as many plant personnel as possible, firing a barrage of questions at everyone from the plant supervisor to the hourly worker. Meanwhile, Gilligan would ask the controller for the company's profit and loss statements for the past half dozen years, and Dameron would evaluate the labor situation.

In looking at potential acquisitions, I tend to value companies the same way I do a new piece of equipment—in terms of how long it should take to pay back the purchase price from earnings. Many people today are using EBITDA (earnings before interest, taxes, depreciation and amortization), but that's a financial guy's measurement. Instead, I always look for payback and cash flow, which I consider an entrepreneur's measurement. Cash flow is your life line, so you had better learn how to calculate and quantify it.

In making our calculations, past performance was never as important to us as perceived potential. For that I came to rely on what Barbee told me about the efficiency of the company's manufacturing process, what Gilligan saw in his financial calculations, Dameron's take on the labor situation, and what my own experience told me could be done to improve the company's bottom line. Sometimes our reasons for rejecting a company were unorthodox, but they were always based on past experience translated into what we felt was simple common sense. One time we passed on a deal after Barbee warned that the company we had visited had morale problems, and that there was evidence of heavy drinking among the plant personnel. How did Barbee know? He had noticed empty liquor bottles wedged behind the wire mesh protecting the plant's windows.

We always wanted to know the reputation of the company, which we could usually determine with a few phone calls. We asked ourselves whether it had a powerful brand, and if the company's financials were in line with the rest of the industry. And finally, we tried to find out *why* a company was for sale. Was it because the entire industry was in trouble? Was a competitor taking it to the cleaners? Or was there a more positive reason from our point of view? Perhaps the owners wanted to take their money out after a lifetime of building the company, or they felt the need to become part of a larger company in order to compete in the marketplace.

Ultimately, the choice of which companies to investigate, and then which to buy, rested more on our instincts than on any quantifiable evaluation. Gulf and Western reportedly had a major bank do much of its legwork, and Litton Industries used one of the Big Five auditors. That worked well for them, but I would be careful about relying too much on consultants. You and your direct reports, not the consultants, will ultimately have to operate any acquisition profitably. We, of course, could afford no such luxuries anyway. Instead, the four of us flew into a site, looked around, and if we liked what we saw, if the industry fit one of our nucleuses, and if we felt the purchase price was fair, we made the deal.

I did not have the desire, or the clout with the banks or Wall Street, to engage in public fights for control of companies. We also purposely avoided getting ourselves into a situation in which we were expected to dictate the price. You have to assume that most companies for sale are overpriced. My attitude was that if the price is comparable to what other companies in that same industry have sold for, then the only important determination was whether or not we could recoup the cost of the purchase price from profits in a reasonable period of time.

My payback calculations may be slightly different than most, however, particularly for what we called "tuck-in" acquisitions. Many times we purchased a company in order to add a new product or expertise. I calculated payback for an acquisition based on the earnings of the new combined company, since the reason we had made the acquisition in the first place was to help the entire nucleus.

I tried never to come in with a predetermined price. Once, an owner told me he didn't know anything about valuing a company and begged us to name a price that we considered fair. When we got back to him with a number, he told us he thought he could get twice that amount elsewhere. I had broken my own rule, so shame on me. We never acquired that company, and as far as I know the owner never sold it.

When there was a wide difference of opinion about how much a company was worth, we would either walk away from the deal, or would offer an earn-out over a period of years based on future performance. In that way if the company performed as well as the owners predicted, they would eventually get their price, while if it didn't perform up to expectations, they would not.

In early 1973, for example, I was in London negotiating to buy Fred Perry Sportswear, named after the three-time Wimbledon champion. We had been told by our British financial advisor that we could buy any company in Great Britain for six times earnings. But the owners of Fred Perry were asking twice that and wouldn't budge. "I thought you said I could buy any company in England for six times earnings," I said to our advisor.

"Any company but Fred Perry," he told us.

We ended up basing the purchase price on six times earnings, but building in a five-year earn-out plan that would give the owners their requested value if the company performed as well they were predicting. Neither side ever had any reason for regret, as both sales and profits at the division tripled during the next decade.

We tried to be creative in other ways as well. During our negotiations with Russ Duncan, chairman of American LaFrance's parent company, he assured us that talks with the union were going well and that he expected to agree on a raise of only ten cents per hour. But people on the manufacturing floor were telling Barbee and

Gilligan otherwise. We had negotiated a purchase price, but now we insisted that the company put $250,000 into an escrow account to protect us against the possibility of a strike. The following year, after labor negotiations had stalled and a strike was in fact called, the funds helped us survive a few rough months at LaFrance.

Sometimes our acquisition strategy was less than scientific. One of our most successful acquisitions came about because I was having trouble ordering the right Rusco storm windows for the house my wife, Nancy, and I were building in the suburbs of Cleveland. When I asked Mary to get the president of Rusco on the phone for me, she mistakenly put the call through to Robert Fox, president of Rusco Industries in Glendale, California. I started going on and on about the problems I was having with my storm windows. Finally Fox explained that he didn't have much to do with the window end of the business, which was located in New Jersey. He ran the Rusco Electronics Systems division, a manufacturer of electronic card-controlled security access equipment. It so happened we were looking for technology companies for our fire protection and security nucleus, and a few months later we bought Rusco Electronics. Fox remained the division's president until his retirement ten years later.

> Negotiation style can be more important than the dollars you offer or the accounting methods you bring into play.

Personal Approach to Negotiation

I think our style of negotiation was more important than the numbers we were offering or the accounting methods we brought into play. Many of the owners we were negotiating with were the entrepreneurial founders of their respective companies. In many cases they wanted to sell their company, but also to maintain their position as president, at least until they retired. They felt a responsibility to their employees to make a deal that would have the company continue to operate independently even after they were out of the picture.

I was well aware that giving up ownership was probably the

most important thing these men would ever do in their business lives. I went out of my way to assure them that the sale of their company was not only good for them and their families financially, but would ultimately be good for the company and its employees. Particularly when negotiating with entrepreneurial founders, I felt it was to our advantage that I was the one sitting across the negotiating table from them. I wanted them to understand that this was an important transaction for us too, and that we were counting on them to be an important part of something bigger than their company alone.

We touted this commitment to entrepreneurship in our public pronouncements, in our annual reports, even in the legal documents we drafted when making an acquisition. For years the back of Automatic Sprinkler stationery stated company philosophy, including the declaration that it was "a corporation of entrepreneurs" and that "division presidents have the decision-making authority to run their companies." This would be a key ingredient of our success during the next three decades.

I think this commitment gave us an advantage over other suitors. Our interest in retaining current management and allowing them to operate their company independently was appealing to many owners. It was also good business. The personnel at the companies we acquired were the most important asset we were buying. We had to be careful not to alienate them. A mass exodus of employees at one division could prove disastrous for an already thinly stretched corporate staff. We were continually striking a balance between jumping right into a new acquisition to make certain its management took the steps necessary to improve profitability, and allowing them to utilize their expertise to the fullest. They knew their company better than we did; we just wanted to add our own expertise to the mix. Sometimes it was a difficult balance to maintain, but it was crucial to our growth plans.

> Ask the old owners to stick with you, to be an important part of something bigger than their company alone.

Unless we were using it as a tuck-in acquisition, or were interested only in a particular product line, we wouldn't even consider buying a company if management didn't agree to stay. They knew their company better than anyone we could bring in. We regarded them as an important asset, and were eager to make certain they stayed with us.

> One of the biggest problems a maturing company has is retaining its entrepreneurial flair. The back of our stationery stated that we were a corporation of entrepreneurs, and that division presidents had the decision-making authority to run their companies.

Retaining current management, advising them in such areas as cost reduction and labor negotiations, but allowing them to run their own entrepreneurial enterprise without heavy corporate overhead, was a key ingredient in the internal growth of Figgie International. Early acquisitions like Automatic Sprinkler, Snorkel (telescopic ladders for fire trucks), Scott Aviation (oxygen equipment), and Interstate Electronics (submarine instrumentation systems) had twenty percent annual growth during the 1970s and '80s. In fact, one of the biggest problems we had was retaining that entrepreneurial flair as we matured into a large company. We tried to do it by offering a compensation plan that included generous incentive bonuses for excellent performance, and by offering people the opportunity to build a business. But I think our most effective weapon was to get them excited about being part of a growing, vibrant corporate enterprise.

> Strike a balance between jumping right into a new acquisition to improve profitability, and allowing current management to utilize their expertise to the fullest.

Goon Squad

Even while giving division presidents a lot of independence, we also knew we had to improve performance if we expected our building block strategy to work. While Gilligan and I were acquiring a company a month, it fell to Barbee to make improvements in those companies we had recently purchased. Many of our early acquisitions were ailing companies either losing money at the time of their purchase or operating with extremely low margins. In order to quickly improve profitability, Barbee's team of industrial engineers would often enter a plant and work with management to make certain our stringent cost reduction measures were implemented. When necessary, Barbee and his industrial engineers would stay at a new acquisition until a problem was solved or a facility was operating efficiently. They thought nothing of sitting in a hotel room until early morning trying to figure out how to change a process or reorder a procedure. As the corporation grew, Barbee only went to the trouble spots, staying away from those divisions that were operating smoothly. It was a decade before he set foot in Scott Aviation's facilities outside of Buffalo, for example. On the other hand, Barbee seemed to take up residency at each of those divisions having difficulties. His job was to solve problems, and he doggedly stayed at a plant until the red ink changed to black. Gilligan and I didn't like to say Uncle. Barbee would never say it.

The Badger Fire Extinguisher Company became the second target for turnaround, after Automatic Sprinkler itself. But unlike with Automatic, Jim Gilligan and I were too busy identifying and investigating the acquisition opportunities that were beginning to flood the office to duplicate the time and effort we had devoted to Automatic Sprinkler. Badger thus became the first challenge for the group of industrial engineers headed by Len Barbee, a group Barbee labeled the "Goon Squad."

The Goon Squad entered the Badger plant in Ranson, West Virginia and immediately began to investigate why the company, which had a solid market share and a respected product, was not profitable. Prices were raised, and Barbee put a halt to the company's practice of giving away one fire extinguisher for every dozen it sold. New employees were added in the accounting, sales, and production departments, paid for by cost reduction measures in the manufacturing and purchasing areas. After we went public, cash was made available to modernize the production facilities and establish a full-time research and development department. A new assembly operation was opened in Charlottesville, Virginia, and the size of the plant in West Virginia was doubled and equipped with state-of-the-art facilities for high volume production.

During the second half of 1964, just before we acquired it, Badger had lost a whopping $74,376 on sales of only $148,850. In 1966 sales increased two hundred and sixty percent compared to a year earlier, and profits tripled. After three years, we were recovering the purchase price every quarter.

American LaFrance was another trouble spot, and Barbee ran it as acting president for fourteen months. Turnover was high, from both layoffs and from the resignations of those who didn't like the changes we were seeking. When a department head resigned, Barbee gave the job to one of his own industrial engineers, with the threat that he would have to stay until he trained a replacement. One summer Barbee rented cabins in the nearby Finger Lakes so that his goon squad could be joined by their families. It was less expensive than paying commuting and hotel costs as the weeks at LaFrance turned into months.

In addition to implementing our cost reduction program, Barbee's industrial engineers installed a new inventory control system and completely revamped LaFrance's assembly procedures. Putting production clocks at key points in the assembly line helped identify the causes of bottlenecks, and a number of time-consuming operations were automated. Daily production tripled. By 1967 sales had jumped more than fifty percent, to $22.8 million, and the company was comfortably in the black.

After closely observing more than five hundred companies, it became evident that there are certain fundamental approaches to reducing costs that transcend virtually all industrial and service organizations.

- Costs can be removed constantly, year after year, within every kind of business, not just manufacturing concerns.
- The people on the front lines are in the best position to suggest and implement cost savings.
- Employees should be given incentives to come up with creative ways to improve profits.
- Concentrate on the most expensive parts, since properly controlling them will lower costs and overhead.
- Work sampling can pinpoint productivity and inefficiency levels of both workers and machines.

Clark Reliance as a Testing Laboratory

The most remarkable aspect of cost reduction efforts aimed at improving profitability is that costs can be removed constantly, year after year. This is true within every kind of business, not just manufacturing concerns. Service organizations, too, become bloated and inefficient over time, and can be streamlined by focusing on those areas where costs are highest.

In fact, people started calling me "the ten percenter" because of our ability to cut costs by ten percent at each of our divisions every year, for three consecutive years. But our efforts went well beyond even that. Profit improvement through cost reduction became a state of mind, a top priority not only for division presidents, but also for every salaried employee. The people responsible for the details of any business operation are in the best position to suggest and implement cost savings in their respective areas. They know better than anyone else about their particular job functions. We took advantage of that by charging all employees with finding and eliminating inefficiencies. We gave them incentives, including bonuses, merit raises, and special prizes, for coming up with creative ways to improve profits.

My sons and I also instilled this kind of focus at our family company, Clark Reliance, which we have owned since the early 1960s.[10] That commitment still remains today. Clark Reliance has orchestrated a cost reduction mindset that keeps constant vigilance on costs by using the same tried and true cost reduction techniques that worked fifty years ago, work today, and should work fifty years from now. The people there understand the importance of focusing on those areas that represent our greatest expenditures. They also pay close attention to their make or buy decisions. Is it less expensive to manufacture a particular part, or is it better to purchase it from an outside supplier? Clark Reliance buys its forgings, for example, from one country and its castings from another, but we do the machining and assembly operations ourselves in Ohio. That is all based on which way costs less money, assuming of course that the quality is identical.

Another important technique is the establishment of an ABC stratification system, whereby all materials and parts are classified into "A," "B," and "C" groupings. Customarily, "C" parts make up seventy-five percent of the total number of items and cause seventy-five percent of outages. They are the literal nuts and bolts of a company's operations—the low dollar, standard, repetitive items that are used most frequently. It pays to keep large reserves of these normally standard items on hand, since they can cause seventy-five percent of shortages. They are inexpensive, and can be bought in great volume once or twice a year, with deliveries staged if desired. "B" parts are the middle group of parts that make up about fifteen to twenty percent of the number of parts that are used and approximately fifteen to twenty percent of the dollars.

"A" parts typically make up seventy to seventy-five percent of the cost of material, but only five to ten percent of the number of

10 Clark Reliance produces a variety of measuring, control, alarm, separation, filtration, and energy conservation equipment for the power and process industries.

parts. They are the most expensive items, and critical to the company's operation. We always want to know how many of these "A" items we have on hand at any given time, and this is where cost reduction efforts in the purchasing area are concentrated. When properly controlled, it is this "A" group that will lower costs and inventory.

The purpose of ABC stratification is to utilize a company's resources on the most important parts. By keeping careful track of "A" parts, an efficient inventory turn can be created. Large amounts of cash won't be tied up in expensive parts waiting idly to be placed into a finished project.

Tried and true methods still work. Even an old reliable work sampling can allow you to take an instantaneous look at any kind of operation, from a machine shop, to an office, to a sales department. By sampling the frequency and effectiveness of activity at the various work stations, work sampling can pinpoint productivity and inefficiency levels of both workers and machines. It measures work pace, as well as quality. Quality improvements reduce waste and rejection, which lessens purchasing, tooling, and handling costs.

The Incredible

At Automatic Sprinkler, we worked inside a constant buzz of activity, with the phone always ringing, something always happening, a crisis always waiting to be solved. Sometimes it felt like Gilligan, Barbee, Dameron, and I were spending more time hanging around airports waiting for yet another connecting flight than either inspecting potential acquisitions or, better yet, sleeping soundly in our own beds. Often the plants we wanted to inspect were located in out-of-the-way spots not serviced by regular commercial airlines. When Sprinkler's board of directors asked what they could do to help, we replied in unison: "Please buy us an airplane."

It was years before the novelty of having a corporate jet of our very own wore off. Suddenly at a moment's notice we could visit any city or plant we liked, no matter how inaccessible. But first we felt we ought to give our sparkling new flying machine a name.

Most of the early principals of the new Automatic Sprinkler Corporation of America were Midwesterners. There was an inside joke among upwardly mobile Midwestern businessmen that if we were successful in our endeavors, one of the benefits would be the ability to send our children to college in the East, where our children would be taught to say *incredible* instead of *bullshit.* Thus one of our directors dubbed Automatic Sprinkler's first corporate airplane *Incredible*. Subsequent planes were named *Incredible II*, *Incredible III*, up to about *Incredible VIII*.

By the time the original *Incredible* was sold in 1973 it had logged more than five thousand air hours, or about two million miles, mostly during the first three years we owned it. It would be impossible to fly two million miles without experiencing a few close calls. One morning we had just taken off for Omaha when we heard a loud "Thump. Thump. Thump." One sea gull after another had bounced off *Incredible's* left wing. Miraculously, none of the birds had flown into the engine, although our pilot, Harry Rees, found part of a sea gull draped across the antenna. We were later told that a dozen carcasses were found strewn along the runway at Lakefront Airport.

Another time at thirty-five thousand feet I heard a loud crack coming from the cockpit. I poked my head in to see a gaggle of cracks covering the windshield. It looked like it had a thousand cracks in it, but our chief pilot assured us it would hold. Nonetheless, we cut our trip short and flew commercially back that night. The windshield became a coffee table in my office.

I don't smoke or drink (I smoked cigars in the Army to keep my hands warm), and set a fairly businesslike tone to our travels. But that didn't mean there wasn't a steady stream of hard-edged kidding and practical jokes in the office, in the air, and on the road. From the very start I sat in the right front seat, just behind the cockpit. The chair diagonally across from me was dubbed the "needle seat," because whoever was sitting in it invariably spent the flight being grilled about one problem or another. It got to the point where the other passengers, in the company's own version of musical chairs, would arrive at the airport earlier and earlier in order to avoid sitting there. That meant it became Barbee's regular seat.

Barbee also took the brunt of most of the needling. One time we had stopped in Detroit so Dale Coenen could catch a commercial flight back to New York. The original *Incredible's* bathroom facilities were not very comfortable, and Barbee told us that it would just take a minute for him to run into the terminal and use the men's room. But it was late, and everyone was tired and eager to get back to Cleveland. The plane was parked on the edge of the runway, so Barbee compromised by stepping out the door and unzipping his fly.

Moments later, on the cockpit radio, chief pilot Harry Rees heard the pilot of a Northwest Airlines jet say, "Tower, there's a man out there. We're ready to move and he's right in front of us. What's he doing?"

All of a sudden the Northwest Captain flipped on his landing lights, exposing Barbee for all the world to see.

When it wasn't Barbee, it was Mary who was typically the object of the practical jokes. She lived with her aunt, who had raised both her and her sister. Suddenly she found herself spending twelve hours a day in close proximity to men who didn't mince words when trying to get our point across, especially when talking with each other. Particularly Len, but Gilligan too, even in the most routine conversation, had a tendency to speak in the crude language of overworked manufacturing personnel rather than of pinstriped executives trying to build a Fortune 500 company. During her first few weeks on the job, every time Mary heard us disagree about something she was convinced we'd never talk to each other again, much less be able to work together, and that as a consequence the company would surely fall apart. If Barbee wasn't placing a rubber chicken on her chair, he was putting a poster of Mae West on the wall above her desk with the caption, "Shape up, Mary."

We were a varied lot, but we each had a job to do and counted on each other to do it well. We also were having the time of our lives. This was the beginning of it all, the earliest days when it all lay in front of us. Gilligan, Barbee and I, and sometimes Davis and Harthun, spent 1967 looking at the world from above. We might take off from Cleveland's downtown Lakefront Airport at five in the morning, fly to the west coast for a negotiation or a plant inspection, then make a quick stop in Chicago on the return flight, not landing back at Lakefront until after midnight. Then as dawn broke we would take off for Boston for a meeting with our bankers. Harry Rees thought nothing of being called late at night and having to get out the library of maps he kept by his bed in order to locate some out-of-the-way airport we would be flying into the next morning.

In investigating so many different companies in such a short period of time, we couldn't help but run into a few bizarre situations. It seemed like every week someone was trying to sell us an invention that was going to revolutionize the world, or at least a particular industry. We saw everything from a power fishing reel that could toss a twenty-five pound weight around with ease (in Gilligan's case directly on top of his foot), to an automatic vegetable picker that did a fine job of shaking the grapefruits off the tree but in the process also pulled the trees' roots out of the ground, to a Rube Goldberg-like process which deboned chicken and canned it for sale to the government.

We took to calling these kinds of companies "black box operations" and grew to be leery of them. We would hear about a company with a sophisticated product. The owner would tell us, "Well, we've got this great device, see. It's right here in this black box. It'll do all sorts of weird and wonderful things but we haven't marketed it yet. We'd like to sell you our company. What? You want to know its secrets? Oh no, we couldn't tell you that. You'll have to buy the company first." We learned to spot these too-good-to-be-true companies a mile away.

Despite our hectic schedule, only rarely did the *Incredible* stay away overnight. Nancy was taking care of the home front, but I didn't want to be an absentee father. It helped that my sons and I had baseball in common. We built a field nearby, complete with infield grass, drainage system, and pitching machine. I managed our eldest son's little league baseball team, and later Automatic Sprinkler sponsored Class A amateur teams. On some weekends sixty kids would be practicing in the field. One year we sent six kids to the minors and two of them made it to the major leagues. I was always so grateful to those who had backed our amateur teams during the depression that I made myself a promise that I would do the same if I was ever financially able.

So Far So Good

For Automatic Sprinkler, 1967 was a year that comes along once in a company's lifetime, as eleven more acquisitions propelled sales to $242 million. Earnings after taxes more than doubled, from $4.4 million to $9.2 million. Sales, profits, and our stock price were all at record highs. *Business Week* called us a "fireball on the acquisition front." On October 2 we confirmed our evolution from an ailing, unwanted fire sprinkler company to a legitimate growth company when our traded shares were transferred from the Over the Counter market to the New York Stock Exchange. The board of directors celebrated the event with a number of us arriving at the Stock Exchange on an American LaFrance hook and ladder truck. The stock celebrated by jumping another sixty-five percent during the last two months of the year.

CHAPTER FOUR

Growth from Within

You need confidence when you're building a $1 billion corporation from scratch.

Eventually, every acquiring company has to stop, consolidate what it has purchased, and prove that it can make a profit all by itself.

EARLY ONE WINTER MORNING IN LATE 1967 a particularly nasty wind blew off Lake Erie, zeroing into the faces of Jim Gilligan, Lou Harthun, and our outside counsel, Al Sommer[11], as they ran up the steps and took refuge inside the Incredible. They were on their way to Washington, D.C., where they would be met by Dick Boland, the Arthur Anderson partner in Cleveland in charge of the Automatic Sprinkler account. The four men had an appointment at the Securities and Exchange Commission to contest a preliminary ruling that had disallowed the accounting method we had used to acquire Blazeguard, a small New Jersey fire hose manufacturer.

At the meeting, Boland and Sommer did most of the talking. They politely but firmly explained our point of view to the examiner, a man by the name of Hodge. But Hodge was adamant. "Absolutely

11 Al would later serve on our board of directors until his appointment as an SEC Commissioner in 1974.

not," he told them. "There's no precedent for the way you want to do this. It's exactly like the Paradine case." The arguments went back and forth for the better part of an hour. "It's exactly like the Paradine case," Hodge kept insisting.

Suddenly Gilligan, who had hardly said a word the entire meeting, slapped his hand on the table, the sound of hand against wood reverberating inside the small office. All eyes went to Gilligan as the room went silent. "The hell it's like the Paradine case!" he bellowed.

Sommer's and Harthun's jaws dropped, but Gilligan just glared at Hodge. Hodge finally broke the silence by confidently asking his legal assistant to bring him the citation for the Paradine case. A few minutes later the SEC lawyer sheepishly admitted that Gilligan was right. The Paradine case did in fact support Automatic's position. Hodge had no choice but to allow us to record the Blazeguard acquisition as planned.

As the Automatic Sprinkler men exited the building Harthun turned to Gilligan and asked him how in the world had he known that the Paradine case supported their position. None of the others had ever even heard of the Paradine case.

"I never heard of it either," Gilligan shrugged. "But I didn't trust that guy Hodge. I figured I'd take a chance on a bluff. We were going down the tubes on something we dearly needed and there was only one way to rescue it, and that was to force the guy to prove he was right. Instead, he proved he was wrong."

Jim's actions typified our modus operandi during these early years. We were focused solely on results, and with each new success our confidence swelled. We believed we could achieve anything we set out to do, whether it was acquire a company at our price, get a bank loan, or convince the SEC that our strategies were sound. This is the kind of confidence you need when you're building a $1 billion corporation from scratch, the kind of confidence that had allowed us to buy a perennial money loser and in twelve months turn it around, and then to do the same with a series of other marginal operations. It was an attitude that helped build Automatic Sprinkler into what by the end of 1967 was a twenty-six-division diversified company with sales of close to a quarter of a billion dollars, a long way from our $23 million origins.

Don't Take Anything For Granted

Suddenly, however, the spell wore off. Perhaps we should have sensed something ominous in the air when in November 1967 the bizarre rumor began to circulate that I had died. Like most rumors, it was impossible to pinpoint its source. Or perhaps our corporate advertisement portraying the fictional Figgie Tool and Dye Works on a tombstone was misinterpreted. Or maybe it was started by someone who had sold our stock short. Whatever the reason, people began calling our corporate offices demanding to know the nefarious purpose that must explain why Automatic Sprinkler had delayed making a public announcement confirming that Harry Figgie had passed away.

Fortunately, it was a simple rumor to put to rest. I scheduled meetings with business reporters, security analysts, and bankers in Cleveland, Boston, and New York. As I walked to the podiums in each city I tried putting a special buoyancy to my gait before paraphrasing Mark Twain with the announcement that rumors of my death had been exaggerated. I actually circulated copies of a handwritten letter from my personal physician attesting to my good health.

But this was the least of our problems, and the easiest to dispel. Suddenly we began to have serious problems at several important divisions. At Interstate Engineering, a court-ordered change in the way it sold its vacuum cleaners and home fire alarms cost us about $600,000 in profits. Delays in opening our new foundry at Powhatan Brass (a manufacturer of brass fittings) caused profits there to temporarily disappear as well. At Kersey Manufacturing (electrical vehicles), sales volume experienced a sharp decline due to industry-wide strikes which virtually shut down the nation's coal production. And at Automatic Sprinkler, still our largest and most profitable division, two days before its contract with Local 1638 of the United Steelworkers of America was due to expire, the hourly workers at our Youngstown headquarters walked out on strike.

> Sometimes you have to take a stand even if it puts your company at risk.
>
> You can't be competitive if your labor costs are significantly higher than your competitors.
>
> Whenever someone says to me, "do this or else," I'm inclined to shake hands on the "or else."

Youngstown Strike

Labor trouble had been brewing for years at Sprinkler, mainly because the former owners had agreed to base wages on the steel industry, rather than on those offered by our competitors in the sprinkler business, most notably Grinnell, the largest sprinkler manufacturer in the country. I had made a strategic decision, and wasn't trying to hide it from anyone. We were not in the steel business, and couldn't survive as the only sprinkler company in the United States to pay steelworker wages. During the negotiations we actually laid a copy of Grinnell's most recent union contract on the bargaining table.

But we were hopelessly deadlocked from the start. The union would only discuss the wages paid to their neighbors who belonged to the same union but who for the most part worked for steel companies, while we needed to base our labor cost structure on our competitors in the sprinkler industry.

Sometimes you have to take a stand, even if it puts your company at risk. I was convinced that giving in to the union's demands was actually the riskier strategy. We could not maintain our competitiveness if our labor costs were significantly higher than our competitors.

Almost immediately things turned ugly, as union picketers took control of the main gates. Even a court order "to halt unruly and rough picketing" and affirming our right of access to the plant did not have much effect.

Soon non-union personnel took to sneaking in and out of the plant by crawling underneath a break in the fence. We needed to at least be able to maintain the company's billing and outsourcing departments, not an insignificant portion of Sprinkler's operations. In order to process the paychecks for the company's contract employees scattered across the country on construction jobs, we created a makeshift billing and payroll department at a downtown Youngstown motel.

Once it was clear that we would have to move out of Youngstown, Gilligan and Davis spent Thanksgiving weekend carrying files and office equipment down two flights of stairs, across the railroad tracks, and onto rented trucks. The picketers had sabotaged the gate locks by stuffing the keyholes with garbage, so Davis used a bolt cutter to snap them off. To cover their tracks, he restuffed the new locks with paper.

One of the most difficult items that had to be removed were the IBM computers, vital to Sprinkler's sales and billing operations. Today comparable equipment could be carried easily by one person, but in 1967 it was a huge electronic monster. Somehow Gilligan located the company's three IBM servicemen at a formal dinner party and convinced them, still in tuxedos, to crawl under the fence with him to help retrieve the computers safely.

Lou Harthun was also busy, subletting space in the Rockefeller building in downtown Cleveland and purchasing furniture to supplement what would be arriving from Youngstown. He and Henry Knippenberg, who we had recently hired as director of Corporate Planning, spent the weekend in a rented truck, traveling from one used furniture store to another where they would point to desks and chairs and filing cabinets and tell the delighted store owners, "I'll take eight of those, three of those, six of those, two of ...."

For the next seventeen months, eighty to one hundred office employees made the three hour round-trip commute from Youngstown to Cleveland in three chartered Greyhound buses. As for the plant, I gave Barbee ten days to come up with three possible replacements from which to choose. A week later we visited a facility in Swainsboro, Georgia, and immediately purchased it.

I think the union never thought we would actually close down the Youngstown facility. They never really believed that at the end of the day we would risk our most important division by laying out the substantial startup costs necessary to move it elsewhere. But the union continued to insist that since Automatic Sprinkler was located in the steel valley, it would have to pay steelworker wages or else. Whenever someone says to me, "do this or else," I'm inclined to shake hands on the "or else."

Finally we acquired a company with problems so severe that even our profit improvement magic couldn't solve them.

Baifield

Thus far, none of the divisional problems that had adversely affected our earnings could really be termed serious. Interstate and Powhatan were both solid companies that would soon return to long-term profitability. Even our costly move out of Youngstown was a one-time expense that would soon be more than recouped by the substantial savings it produced. But then finally we acquired a company with problems so severe that even our profit improvement magic couldn't solve them.

On the surface, Baifield Industries seemed like an ideal acquisition. It had a reliable customer in the U.S. Defense Department, and had never made less than ten percent on any contract. Mainly due to the escalation of the Vietnam War, its sales had jumped from $9.1 million in 1964, to $15.4 million in 1965, to $31.3 million in 1966.

But problems arose soon after the acquisition was finalized. Baifield had just signed a $6 million contract with the federal government to manufacture drawn casings for 105-millimeter armor-piercing shells. After a supplier backed out of its contract to provide the steel, Baifield began importing steel from Europe. This was a crucial mistake. We were already having serious problems with the reliability of the government-furnished equipment, and should have known that any variance in the steel would only make matters worse. It's common knowledge that European steel is more acidic than American steel, and therefore travels through forging machinery differently. We should have insisted that the current supplier, a major U.S. steel company, honor its contract.

Barbee and several of his industrial engineers spent the better part of the year at the Baifield plant in Shreveport, Louisiana, vainly trying to "squeeze orange juice from banana peels," as Barbee put it. He was making progress until demand for the "Snakeye," responsible for most of Baifield's revenue, suddenly evaporated. The "Snakeye" was a fin-like device that slowed the flight of bombs falling from rapid, low-flying planes, delaying impact and enabling pilots to escape a target area before the bombs exploded. But U.S. aircraft, flying low to the ground so they could accurately attack the supplies being brought overland from China on the Ho Chi Min Trail, were becoming increasingly vulnerable to anti-aircraft fire. In order to protect the lives of its pilots, the U.S. military began using only high-flying planes firing computer-guided missiles.

As a result, in one year Baifield's sales volume fell from $45 million to less than $8 million, and in 1970 the division disappeared altogether. The drain on our overall company was severe. In 1968 our second quarter net profit was an almost invisible $215,000, compared to $3.8 million a year earlier. For the year, sales jumped to $325 million, up from $242 million, but earnings per share plummeted to ten cents, down from $1.43.

Our stock price took a beating as well. In three years it had soared from $20 a share to $73, even after a five for two split, but then virtually overnight it sank back down to $25 and was rapidly on its way to single digits. The bearish stock market did not help matters. In June 1969 the Dow Jones Average dipped under 900, and closed the year under 800. In May 1970 it finally bottomed out at 631.

> Our biggest challenge was to improve cash flow and debt-to-equity levels by keeping working capital under control.

Take a Breath

By the close of the 1960s, conglomerates had fallen out of favor on Wall Street, and without a high stock price, the rapid acquisitions of the previous five years were a thing of the past. But I had never intended to grow by acquisition indefinitely anyway. We were one conglomerate that did not have to depend on acquisitions. We were trying to build a solid foundation on which we could grow internally. We were operators; we knew how to turn companies around. Besides, we were never as dependant on a high stock price for making acquisitions as most diversified companies. Typically, we gave owners the choice of taking either stock or cash, trying to find a balance between the two. We had no alternative during those early years than to be highly leveraged, but we nevertheless tried to avoid using stock as wallpaper like some other diversified companies were reportedly doing. At some companies, their stock was called wallpaper because it seemed as if they papered the wall with it. But we tried to keep a balance between our stock and cash acquisitions. It wasn't easy, not with having to operate so many small companies with insatiable appetites for working capital. That was always our biggest challenge—to improve cash flow and debt- to-equity levels by keeping working capital under control.

Future successes would have to come from within, and that fit in perfectly with our long term strategy. In sixty months we had grown from a small private $23 million sprinkler company to a diversified corporation with sales volume in 1968 of $325 million. It was time to consolidate, to improve what we had acquired and to grow from within. After absorbing such a large number of new companies so quickly, it was time to pause from buying companies and concentrate instead on the profitability of the ones we already owned. Our plan was to acquire, consolidate, then acquire once again. This was our consolidation period. The chart on the next page diagrams Figgie International's three phases of growth.

> Our plan was always to acquire, consolidate, then acquire once again.

Figgie International Sales Growth – 1964-1990

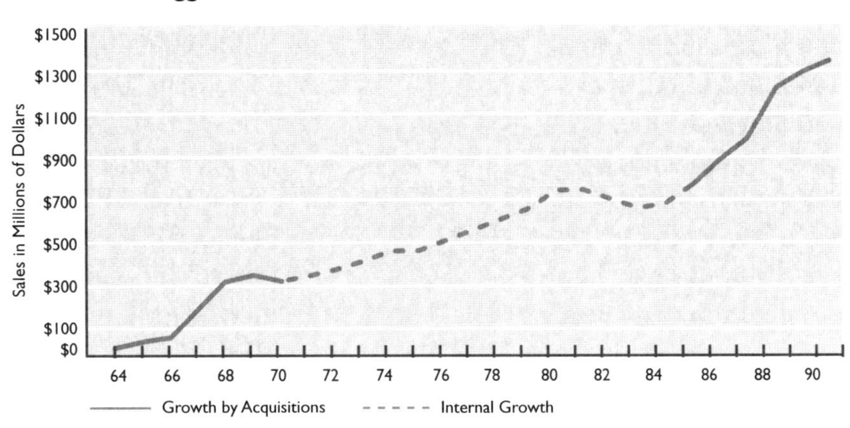

Notes:
Between 1965 and 1969 acquired 51 companies doing $320 milllion in sales, increasing total sales from $22.7 million to $379 million
Between 1970 and 1985 total sales increased from $356 million to $721 million, virtually all of it generated internally
Between 1985 and 1990 total sales increased from $803 million to $1.3 billion; 38 acquisitions cost $194 million

Growing Pains

Certainly we were experiencing growing pains; sure mistakes had been made at Baifield and at a few other divisions. How could we not have made mistakes? In forty-eight months a handful of overworked young executives had acquired almost fifty companies in four business areas and increased our total size by more than three thousand percent.

But I never doubted that we would rebound from our troubles. It was simply another time to roll up our sleeves and get back to work—albeit a different kind of work. If we no longer had the wherewithal to continue acquiring companies, we were perfectly happy to grow from within and try to reduce our debt.

I was bullish on our company, even if Wall Street had soured on us and on diversified companies as a group. None of our problems were by any means insurmountable, and the company as a whole was, in fact, on solid financial footing. I was thankful that the Baifield disaster hadn't occurred earlier, when the company was smaller and could not have stood the jolt. Other divisions, most notably the original Automatic Sprinkler operation, Safway (scaffolding), and Scott Aviation (oxygen masks and other aviation equipment), were reliable cash producers poised for rapid growth. Sales at the Essick (construction equipment) and T. L. Smith (truck mixers) divisions had exceeded expectations, and George Meyer and Speaker Sortations (bottling equipment) both had just experienced one of their best years ever. It was also a good year for the entire sporting goods industry, including Rawlings, which obtained exclusive rights to use all National Football League team names and insignias on its retail line of football clothing and equipment. Our bankers seemed to share our confidence. We were able to arrange a $90 million line of credit from a group of ten banks, only a small portion of which we actually used.

It also helped to have a sense of humor. Once the worst of the Baifield disaster was behind us, Barbee mounted a chrome plated 105 mm shell on a beautiful walnut stand engraved with the words, "Remember Baifield," and gave it to me as a gift. I still have it. And to address the beating we had taken in the press, one of our corporate advertisements was a photograph of me with Band-Aids on my forehead and chin. The caption read: "Our corporation moves so fast it had its 1970 recession in 1968."

> Some consolidations reduce short-term profits, but all of them should aim to eliminate duplications and take advantage of economies of scale.
>
> Gradually adjust your emphasis from growing through acquisitions to building divisions from within.

A New Company Emerges

The goal of our internal growth phase was to boost the annual sales of each division to a minimum of $20-25 million, and each nucleus to more than $100 million. With this in mind, we began to merge operations and close small, unprofitable divisions. We combined Badger, Powhatan, and Blaze Guard (all fire extinguisher divisions), as well as the fire extinguisher unit of American LaFrance, into one unit, renamed Badger-Powhatan. Davis Emergency Equipment was folded into Scott Aviation; General Fittings and Fee and Mason (equipment for heavy machinery) were combined; Omni Lab (a manufacturer of electronic teaching laboratories) was attached to Scott Engineering, and Chatleff Controls (a manufacturer of special purpose valves and controls used primarily in air conditioning and refrigeration systems) to Ward Hydraulics (hydraulic cylinders). Some of these consolidations reduced short-term profits, but all of them eliminated costly duplications and took advantage of our economies of scale.

INTERNAL GROWTH STRATEGIES

- Establish 4-5 groups (nucleuses) each doing $100 million+ in sales, made up of separate divisions each doing $20+ million in sales.
- Accomplish these groupings by merging divisions, consolidating plants, and with "tuck-in" acquisitions."
- Consider the possibility of creating a new division around a single product of an existing division.
- Make each division a profit center headed by an entrepreneurial division president.
- Don't get sentimental. Close or consolidate operations that have not worked out as originally visualized.
- Organize the company with group vice presidents and group controllers who report to the chief executive.
- Create a rigorous annual review and planning process.
- Encourage division presidents to make certain they have their costs under control and have set ambitious yet realistic goals. A simple ratio analysis can reveal the possibilities.
- Balance corporate oversight with entrepreneurial division presidents.
- Periodically examine opportunities to buy back stock, particularly during bear markets.
- Create a corporate identity.
- Develop a long term plan to pay down debt.

Tuck-In Acquisitions

Acquisitions continued to play an important role in our development, but with a crucial difference. Now most of the companies we purchased were what we called "tuck-in" acquisitions, designed to increase the competitive position of an existing division or to increase its size so that it reached one of our minimum divisional sales targets of $20, $50, or $100 million. That was the reasoning behind buying the Toney Penna line of golf clubs and Adirondack baseball bats and merging them into the Rawlings division. Of the twenty companies we acquired in the 1970s, only a half dozen were ever operated as independent divisions, and at least two of those were purchased in order to service the rest of the corporation. For example, in 1970 we acquired Western Reserve Container, a box container company that soon was relying on other divisions for almost a third of its total sales, while at the same time reducing our company's total packaging costs and eliminating certain bottlenecks.

BRAND EXTENSION

Sometimes internal growth can be accomplished by building a new division around a new product. At the end of 1971 we bought Snorkel, a small company that manufactured a telescopic ladder for fire trucks. We were convinced the product could be adapted for the construction industry. We looked into buying JLG Industries, the world's leading producer of what is called "access equipment," including aerial work platforms and telescopic hydraulic excavators. JLG wasn't for sale, so we developed our own product aimed at the construction business. Snorkel's sales quickly jumped from $6 million to more than $30 million, and eventually topped $200 million.

Don't Be Sentimental

Conversely, we were not afraid to close divisions that did not fit into our long-term strategy of 4-5 $100 million+ nucleuses made up of $20 million+ divisions. We either closed or sold about a dozen small divisions, including Blaze Guard (fire hoses), Fee and Mason (pipe hangars), and Hadco-Tiffin (outdoor signs and lockers).

Even the divisions that had been the foundation of our earlier growth were not immune. We took a hard look at American LaFrance and George Meyer, for example. Both these companies were at one time leaders in their industries, but by the 1970s had fallen on hard times and had begun to absorb increasingly large amounts of our corporate cash and attention. We eventually decided to move American LaFrance out of its longtime home in Elmira into a less expensive facility, and as a result it was able to continue to produce fire trucks under its illustrious name.

We took a different approach with George Meyer, which, like other companies in the bottling industry, had seen a drop in sales due to foreign competition. In 1986 we acquired the Mojonnier Corporation. One of Mojonnier's strengths was refrigeration equipment, the one product Meyer had been lacking in order to offer a full line to its customers. Mojonnier also had a large operation in Brazil, boosting our presence in South America. These benefits, along with an across-the-board price increase and an aggressive campaign to streamline the delivery of spare parts, returned George Meyer to profitability.

Corporate Governance

Part of our maturation process during the 1970s was to formalize our nucleus theory into a process by which each nucleus was managed at the corporate level by a group vice president familiar with the overall business, supported by group controllers. Division presidents reported to group vice presidents, who in turn reported to the chief operating officer.

We also had an influx of other personnel, most of them filling newly created positions. Lou Harthun began to assemble a legal staff, a public relations office was established, and executives were actually allowed to hire their own secretaries. A treasurer and controller had already been hired, both of whom were ultimately made corporate vice presidents. Even after taking parts of two floors of the CEI Building, we were bulging at the seams. Three desks in a room, two people to a desk, was not uncommon.

While I concentrated on integrating and growing our existing operations, we hired a president to run day-to-day operations. John Tanis, who had started working for the Automatic Sprinkler division in 1966, became president in 1971, followed by Al Gangnes, who had joined the Interstate Electronics division in 1958. Al had done a superb job for us in straightening out our Interstate division, and then did the same at Scott Aviation. Together Al and I concentrated on developing a cohesive organization, which meant both improving the quality of the personnel at the division level and making sure every division fit into our long-term plans for the corporation.

As part of our effort to integrate all the different divisions, we began to hold annual off-site presidents meetings. I remember the presidents all standing around at the first meeting in Charlottesville, Virginia looking at each other blankly. But as it became a regular event, with our encouragement they began sharing marketing ideas and profit improvement techniques. Every other year spouses were invited.

A New Home for One Company

For years I had dreamed of having a corporate headquarters built in the Colonial Georgian style. Our cramped space at the CEI building notwithstanding, I always felt that once we could afford it, our business environment should be as pleasant as possible. So, in 1968 we paid just over $300,000 for the Sherwin estate, a 106-acre site in the Cleveland suburb of Willoughby, Ohio. It was a beautiful spot, with formal gardens that had been designed by the Olmstead Brothers, who were responsible for New York City's Central Park. We hired Monroe W. Copper, Jr., an architect well known for his early American designs, to build us three Georgian style buildings, which we furnished with art and antiques that fit the period. We later added a computer building, also with an exterior in the Colonial design.

The move to our new headquarters in August 1970 signaled the official end to the hectic days of the past. The new environment, combined with the influx in support staff, was a far cry from Mary, Gilligan, Barbee and me sharing two small rooms. For those of us who had been around since the beginning, there was great satisfaction in having turned fifty different companies into a successful diversified corporation. Instead of running from one problem to the next, we were able to better organize our daily work effort. We started looking at systems and procedures that would benefit the whole rather than just one individual company or group.

But there was also some wistfulness to the memories. The craziness of the sixties had created a bond among a small group of people, all of whom were aware that it had been a once-in-a-lifetime experience. While we were confident that good things would continue to come the company's way, we also knew it would never be the same again, that two million miles in the air, "black box" operations, and closing five deals in twenty-five days were things of the past.

> Hardcore meetings are an important communications link between the divisions and their corporate parent.
>
> Maybe a CEO of a service company can nurture a reputation as being a nice guy. But I don't think that works so well at fledgling manufacturing operations.

Hardcore

Early on we established a system of annual "hardcore" meetings. Every fall each division president and controller met individually with me and the appropriate group officer and controller to outline their plans for the following year, and for the four years after that. I considered there hardcore sessions sacrosanct, a contract between the division president and corporate. In preparation, division presidents were expected to dig into every detail of their business. We would typically choose one particular subject in that vast array of data, and expected a good answer to why something had or had not occurred, not only in the year that the president was projecting, but the current year, and perhaps in the last five years on display, or even five years into the future. Company presidents were expected to know their operations thoroughly, and when they didn't, when they left the planning to their controller, it was generally quite evident in their hardcore presentations.

These hardcore meetings became an important communications link between us at corporate and the divisions. We wanted the presidents to understand that by implementing our standard cost reduction strategies, they could often meet a more ambitious financial performance than they first proposed. At the same time, we were constantly urging them to be realistic about their projections. We wanted them to be confident they could meet their sales and profit projections. We were counting on them to deliver what they promised so we could meet our own cash planning and the estimates we would be making to the financial community. We asked them to be "low task" in their planning and not set unrealistically optimistic goals.

In order to temper their enthusiasm, incentive bonuses were based on hardcore plans. There was no reason for them to overtask, since the compensation of division employees was usually directly related to how well the hardcore projections were fulfilled. Bonuses were directly tied to how much the division exceeded its hardcore projections. Nevertheless, there must have been something psychologically tempting about trying to impress corporate with ambitious projections. We encouraged division presidents to be conservative in their planning, but more often than not, they would overreach and submit a high task plan. It was no wonder that in a typical year only about two-thirds of the divisions met or exceeded their plan.

At one point we were up to forty-three divisions, so I spent a lot of time at these sessions. Some divisions had to revise their hardcore plan several times before it was accepted. But it was worth it. Often they turned into mini profit improvement seminars. Before long, hardcore was looked forward to by those presidents performing well, but dreaded by those who consistently fell short of their projections. If a division president missed his projection two or three years in a row, we would take a hard look at his ability to continue managing that company.

I got a reputation as being tough, even making *Fortune* magazine's 1989 list of toughest bosses in America. But I never apologized for that. Maybe CEOs of service companies can nurture a reputation as being a nice guy. I don't think that works so well at fledgling manufacturing operations. I was trying to make dozens of small, often struggling companies conform to a single set of operating rules and procedures, all aimed at turning a profit. I did not have time to baby any one division, and those who couldn't cut the mustard in this very competitive business environment were gradually replaced, often of their own volition. There were many others, however, who thrived in this environment of entrepreneurial growth. Those people tended to stay with us for many years, many of them rising up the corporate ladder to take on greater responsibilities, in several cases moving from division employee, to division president, to corporate officer.

> Take a look at the lowest ratio of cost as a percentage of sales for each operational category and ask yourself, "What was happening at the company that allowed it to achieve these best results?"
>
> What would the impact be on pretax profits if all the best ratios were achieved during the same year?

Ratio Analysis

During our annual planning meetings, one of our most effective techniques for getting division presidents to set aggressive, yet at the same time realistic, financial goals was to have them perform a ratio analysis of their company. We asked division presidents to bring detailed ratios of their company's operations for the most recent five-year period. At the very least, the categories should include sales, burden (overhead), gross profit, research and development expenditures, cost of debt service, and pretax profits. For each figure, we also asked them to determine their percentage in relationship to sales. Each area was further defined with detailed costs.

Ratio Analysis: The Art of the Possible *(ALL $ IN THOUSANDS)*					
	Year One	Year Two	Year Three	Year Four	Year Five
Sales $	$23,041	$27,923	$31,782	$35,244	**$37,000**
Gross Profit $	$6,642	$7,700	$9,213	$9,675	$10.975
Gross Profit %	28%	27.6%	29%	27.5%	**29.7%**
Selling Expenses $	$3,369	$3,815	$4,539	$5,162	$5,347
Selling Expenses %	14.6%	**13.7%**	14.3%	14.6%	14.5%
G&A Expenses $	$1,212	$1,095	$1,031	$990	$1,069
G&A Expenses %	5.3%	3.9%	3.2%	**2.8%**	2.9%
R&D Expenses $	$133	$182	$143	$196	$214
R&D Expenses %	.6%	.7%	**.4%**	.6%	.6%
Debt Service $	$834	$720	$995	$1,249	$1,122
Debt Service %	2.7%	**2.6%**	3.2%	3.6%	3.0%
Pretax Profit $	$1,087	$1,803	2,504	$2,035	$3,250
Pretax Profit %	4.7%	6.5%	7.7%	5.5%	**8.8%**

In assembling these figures, the goal was to have division presidents take a look at the lowest ratio of cost as a percentage of sales for each operational category. If the best ratios were attained in recent years, that was a sign that the division was improving its performance. Most important, we wanted them to ask themselves how these percentages were achieved. They would invariably discover that all the best ratios had not occurred during the same year. What was happening at that particular division at the time that allowed it to achieve these best results?

It was also instructive for division presidents to take the best of all these ratios and calculate what the pretax profit would have been if they all had been achieved in the same year. They would see that profits would have exceeded anything that was achieved in any single year.

Take a look at the chart on the previous page. In this case, this $37 million company achieved its best gross profit as a percentage of sales during its most recent reporting period. That is obviously a good thing, but the division president could also see that expenses were most effectively kept under control in years two and four. In year two, both selling expenses (13.7 percent) and debt service (2.6 percent) achieved their best (lowest) percentage of sales, and in year four G&A expenses (2.8 percent) had that distinction.

We could also show the division president that if these best percentages were brought to the bottom line, the most recent year's pretax profit could be increased to 10.16 percent. Sales would be $37 million; gross profit, 29.7 percent; selling costs, 13.7 percent; general and administrative expenses, 2.8 percent; debt service, 2.6 percent; and research and development costs, .4 percent.[12]

In an ideal year, therefore, sales would have been $37 million, gross profit $10.975 million, selling costs $5.069 million, G&A $1.036 million, R&D outlays $148,000, and debt service $962,000. These total operating costs (they amount to $7,215,000), when subtracted from gross profit, would have yielded a pretax profit of $3,760,000. Simple arithmetic reveals that pretax profit has improved by 15.7 percent (3,760/3,250), or 10.16 percent of sales.

Ratio analysis teaches that there is no room for complacency. During the last of the five years under review, sales, gross profit, and

12 For the purposes of this exercise, we might actually use an average R&D cost of .6%, recognizing that cutting this category to its lowest percentage is not necessarily advisable.

pretax profit all achieved their highest level for the entire period. Yet a simple macro ratio analysis shows how pretax profit might have been even better.

Profit Attainable Using Lowest Ratios		
Sales	$37 million	
Gross Profit	29.7% =	$10,975,000
Selling Expenses	13.7% =	$5,069,000
G & A Expenses	02.8% =	$1,036,000
R & D Expenses (average)	00.4% =	$148,000
Debt Service	02.6% =	$962,000
Total Expenses		**$7,215,000**
Gross Profit	$10,975,000	
Expenses	$7,215,000	
	$3,760,000 = A pretax profit of 10.16% on sales of $37 million, an improvement over year five's 8.8% pretax profit.	

In a real example, this division president would also put the cost of material, burden, administration and sales expenses, and debt service into a ratio analysis chart to determine in which year the company achieved the lowest costs in each of these categories as a percentage of sales. Every category would then be analyzed further in order to make a more micro determination of individual expense ratios that might be improved.

No matter what independent studies conclude, or how adamant your board of directors, do not ever allow a public company to be named after yourself.

Automatic Sprinkler, to A-T-O, to Figgie International

By 1969 it was obvious that the Automatic Sprinkler Corporation of America name no longer adequately conveyed the scope of our operations. We were much more than a sprinkler company, having by this time extended into labor reduction equipment, fluid controls, defense, and consumer products.

Yet finding a more suitable name wasn't easy. One idea was to select a well-known division, such as Rawlings or American LaFrance, or maybe even a combination like Rawlings/LaFrance, and make it the name of the entire corporation. But that would have only provoked further confusion, since Rawlings and LaFrance made up only a small part of our total sales. Neutral names were also bandied about, such as Automated Industries and Associated Companies of America, but they did not excite any of us.

The Wall Streeters on Automatic Sprinkler's board of directors suggested changing the name to A-T-O, our stock exchange symbol, arguing that everyone knew the corporation as that anyway. A-T-O took on further momentum when "alphabet soup" names became the rage. International Business Machines changed its name to IBM, General Electric to GE, the Radio Corporation of America to RCA, and International Telephone and Telegraph to ITT. So we became A-T-O Inc.

Almost immediately we regretted the decision. A-T-O didn't stand for anything. Insiders liked to joke that it stood for either A Terrific Organization, or Associated Turkeys of Ohio. Outsiders tended to confuse it with the Alpha Tau Omega fraternity and, increasingly, with ATO Chimie, a large French multinational.

But disliking a name was a lot easier than finding a more suitable alternative. For a decade we constantly searched for a more permanent, more powerful replacement. We even ran a contest in our internal corporate newsletter, promising the winner a set of woods from Rawlings Golf. But no one came up with anything that provoked excitement.

Finally, in 1977 A-T-O's board of directors hired a firm that specialized in corporate names to analyze our situation and make a recommendation. They immediately told us what we already knew. The corporation's name was a liability, and we should change it.

Easier said than done. The more than two hundred names submitted by the name change experts, names like Advance International, Interdyne, ATCO, Coactive, the Cohort Corporation, Multicog, Combex, and the Multistar Corporation, were as meaningless as the one we were already using. True, other companies were succumbing to the suggestions of their consultants and taking on strange sounding names with nice rings to them. American Can became Primerica, Burroughs and Sperry became Unisys, Libbey-Owens-Ford became Trinova, and International Harvester became Navistar International. But to us, names like these were just sounds that failed to suggest our business or philosophy. We were a company on the move, having grown from $19 million in 1963, to $358 million in 1971, to $628 million in 1978. I agreed that we needed a name that would provoke excitement, and create a strong identity for a company that had been one of the top financial performers of the 1960s and '70s.

I should have kept my mouth shut. It was at this point that one of our directors, Bob Weaver, came up with the idea of naming the company Figgie International, and he quickly convinced the other board members that this was the one name that made sense. For better or worse, I was identified with A-T-O. What better way to give the company a personality?

Bob initiated an internal campaign to gather support for his position, writing letters to the board and lobbying the executive committee. Still, I was reluctant, so we hired a New York research company to conduct a survey asking business journalists, business school deans, and personnel managers of Fortune 500 companies their attitudes toward naming corporations after individuals. A group of financial analysts were asked similar questions, and queried in order to determine their ability to recognize ten specific corporations and their CEOs. According to the study, sixty-one percent of the "business leaders" and seventy-nine percent of the financial analysts agreed with the statement, "a comparatively meaningless name, such as Acme or A-T-O, contributes to the anonymity of a company." "I think acronym-like names are an insult to the English language," one financial editor was quoted as saying.

Financial analysts were also asked to name the first thing that came to mind after hearing each of ten different companies—A-T-O, Dart, Chrysler, Parker-Hanifin, General Motors, IBM, Fuqua, General Electric, Westinghouse, and Warner & Swasey. One-third of the analysts responded "Harry Figgie" when A-T-O was mentioned, by far the highest percentage for any chief executive. This did not mean I was the best known CEO, only that I was most identified with the company where I worked. When asked to match the ten CEOs with their companies, I ranked third, after John Riccardo of Chrysler and J.B. Fuqua of Fuqua Industries.

Another part of the study was conducted at Columbia University's Business School. Two versions of a mock front page of the *New York Times* business section were prepared. One version contained an article about A-T-O, while the other contained the identical article, except the company was called the "Figgie Group." The articles were distributed to five business school classes, 202 students in all. Half the students were given the A-T-O version and half the Figgie version, with the Figgie version prompting significantly higher recall.

On May 20, 1981 a shareholders vote officially changed A-T-O, Inc. to Figgie International, Inc.

No matter what independent studies conclude, or how adamant your board of directors, don't ever allow yourself to be convinced to name a public company after yourself. Nancy and I are private people. Now suddenly our name was thrust into the headlines. Every time Figgie International hiccupped, it seemed like I personally had a major bellyache. Figgie did this or Figgie did that, blared headlines all over the country, not making any distinction between Figgie the man and Figgie the company.

> Our division presidents had the decision-making authority to run their own companies.
>
> Maintaining the independence of divisions allows a diversified corporation to take advantage of its entrepreneurial roots.

A Company of Entrepreneurs

At the same time that we were exerting control at the corporate level, we also wanted division presidents to maintain as much autonomy as they could handle. From the very outset, we made a concerted effort to allow each division to operate independently, at least until it proved it could not do so profitably or was not implementing our cost cutting guidelines. We remained sensitive to a division's desire to remain autonomous, while at the same time impressing upon each division president the corporation's need to make important changes that would improve profitability.

We wanted to take advantage of those divisions, like Automatic Sprinkler, Rawlings, Fred Perry Sportswear, Tony Penna, and Scott Aviation, that had well known brands in their respective fields. We also felt that maintaining the independence of divisions was the way our diversified corporation could operate most successfully. Our small corporate staff couldn't possibly understand a division's business as well as the people who had been working there for years, sometimes for all their professional lives. Those divisions doing well received little corporate counseling, while those performing poorly received our undivided attention. This allowed us to jump into the most severe problem areas when necessary.

Indeed, one of our most important criteria in choosing the companies we purchased was the quality of the people in charge. During our internal growth phase that strategy really paid off. We were determined to pay more than lip service to our boast that we were a company of entrepreneurs, that division presidents enjoyed a large degree of autonomy and had the decision-making authority to run their own companies. We wanted to find out as soon as possible who could be counted on, so we gave them the opportunity to prove their worth by making difficult decisions on their own, even if that meant making some mistakes. Gilligan liked to say, "We give our division presidents so much rope that in the end they have to either hang themselves, or use the rope to keep us out."

We also tried to establish a competitive environment that rewarded financial achievement. In addition to our regular bonus system tied to division, group, and corporate profits, we presented an Outstanding Performance Award each year to one large and one small division that had excelled in profit achievement, cost reduction, growth, and product development. We instituted a tag-along program, in which middle-management employees learned the ropes by "tagging along" with a senior level executive for a few weeks. And corporate officers spent three months at Harvard's Advanced Management Program in order to broaden their decision-making and planning skills.

Investing In Ourselves

Despite sales, profits, and earnings per share that indicated we had turned the corner away from the problems we had experienced in late 1960s, our stock continued to nosedive. To some extent it was self-fulfilling. The media tended to ignore our healthy divisions and focus almost exclusively on our trouble spots, like Baifield. Wall Street followed suit. Most analysts at the time weren't interested in diversified companies, mainly because they were difficult for a single person to understand. Analysts tend to specialize in a particular industry, and feel most comfortable following companies that are growing within that specialty. As a result, each analyst might have a good handle on one of our nucleuses; it was the rare analyst who had a good handle on our entire business.

But since I did not need it for acquisitions, our low stock price didn't worry me. In fact, I looked at this period as an opportunity for us to reduce the number of shares outstanding. On several occasions during the 1970s and eighties the corporation bought back its shares on the open market in order to reduce the number of our common shares by about twenty-five percent. For the short term, the buybacks increased our debt and were a drain on profits. But we made the long-term decision that it was important to balance stock buybacks and debt reduction. We eventually would be rewarded when in the mid-1980s the stock finally began to rise again, topping $70 per share.

CHAPTER FIVE

Beware of Debt

We should insist that the federal government apply the same straightforward fiscal philosophy to its own finances that shareholders expect public corporations to maintain.

"The same prudence which in private life would forbid our paying our own money for unexplained projects forbids it in the dispensation of the public moneys... we must not let our rulers load us with perpetual debt."

—Thomas Jefferson

THOSE OF US ON THE GROUND FLOOR of Figgie International considered our rise from a small, struggling fire sprinkler company to a *Fortune* 500 diversified corporation proof that our economic system works, that in America a team of people with little more than a dream and hard work can be successful. We were humbled by the experience. We knew how fortunate we were to have created a large company from scratch during a period in America of great opportunity for entrepreneurs. I don't think we could have done what we did in any other country in the world.

I hope that in some small way this book will encourage prospective entrepreneurs to do something similar. There is absolutely no reason why a young person today could not do precisely what we did—begin with a solid nucleus and build it into a *Fortune* 500 company by buying small companies and turning them around through aggressive profit improvement. In fact, this type of growth strategy is easier today than it ever was. The internet makes finding companies that fit your particular criteria much easier, whether you are looking for a certain company size or area of business. And low interest rates, combined with the proliferation of both venture capital firms and aggressive pension plans, have increased the availability of money with which to acquire leveraged businesses.

A New Problem

There is one serious caveat to this optimism, however. We were able to accomplish what we did by keeping our eyes on the ball, by following basic economic principles that guide any good businessman: Be frugal. Spend wisely so you make a profit. Pay very close, constant attention to cash flow, debt-to-equity ratios, and spending. And most important of all, don't spend what you don't have. I have spent my business life trying to encourage my companies, and my country, to follow these very simple, unalterable rules. When Figgie International stopped following them while I was in a hospital bed for fifteen months, the company imploded. Now I fear the same lack of discipline threatens to provoke similar consequences for our very way of life in the United States.

We grew Figgie International from $23 million to $1.3 billion in an environment that encouraged entrepreneurship, but also sound business principles. There was a general acknowledgement that companies, as well as countries, should not spend more than they take in. That may seem self evident, but somewhere along the way many people, including those who control the U.S. federal government, decided that these rules no longer applied.

But they do apply, and they always will. If the federal government continues to accept higher and higher deficits, I fear a positive business environment, particularly for entrepreneurs, could evaporate.

Deficit spending by the United States government is a relatively new phenomenon, and an extremely troublesome one, no matter what the politicians would have us believe. For the country's first 183 years, it accumulated a total debt of $310 billion, or an average of $1.7 billion per year.[13] For the most part, the government operated on a pay-as-you-go basis. Expenditures equaled revenue. If it needed to spend more, it raised revenues, most typically through taxes. It was understood that the only time the government would borrow substantial sums would be during wartime.

But then came Lyndon Johnson, who managed to finance two simultaneous wars—one against the North Vietnamese in Southeast Asia, and another at home against poverty in America—without raising taxes or reducing any other expenses. He did it by borrowing, and deficits began their inexorable march, from a scant $1.4 billion in 1965, to $25.2 billion in 1968, to $73.7 billion in 1976, to $221.2 billion in 1986, to $290.3 billion in 1992.

I was so concerned about this trend that fifteen years ago I sat down to write, with University of Arizona Economics Professor Gerry Swanson, *Bankruptcy 1995*. It was written during a financial environment similar to what we have now, when interest on the national debt was the largest item in the federal budget, topping even the enormous Pentagon and Social Security budgets. It must have struck a nerve, because the book remained on the *New York Times* bestseller list for more than nine months.

The dot.com phenomenon allowed us to briefly balance the federal deficit under President Clinton, but once that bubble burst deficits began to rise once again, until in recent years the situation has deteriorated even further. Deficits are now currently running at the highest in our history. In 2005, $352 billion was spent just on interest payments to service our government's debt, and the national debt is increasing at a rate of about $1.7 billion—every day![13]

America has become a country with a champagne appetite and a beer income. For every dollar the government collects in taxes, it is

13 All deficit figures are taken from data published by the White House Office of Management and Budget.

Annual Deficit/Surplus by Presidential Administration

(IN MILLIONS) SOURCE: OFFICE OF MANAGEMENT AND BUDGET

Between 1781 and 1963 the cumulative debt was $310 billion

LYNDON JOHNSON

1964	-5.9
1965	-1.4
1966	-3.7
1967	-8.6
1968	-25.2

RICHARD NIXON

1969	+3.2
1970	-2.8
1971	-23.0
1972	-23.4
1973	-14.9
1974	-6.1

GERALD FORD (IN BILLIONS)

1975	-53.2
1976	-73.7

JIMMY CARTER

1977	-53.7
1978	-59.2
1979	-40.7
1980	-73.8

RONALD REGAN

1981	-79
1982	-128
1983	-207.8
1984	-185.4
1985	-212.3
1986	-221.2
1987	-149.7
1988	-155.2

GEORGE H.W. BUSH

1989	-152.6
1990	-221
1991	-269.2
1992	-290.3

BILL CLINTON

1993	-255.1
1994	-203.2
1995	-164
1996	-107.4
1997	-21.9
1998	+69.3
1999	+125.6
2000	+236.2

GEORGE W. BUSH

2001	+128.2
2002	-157.8
2003	-377.6
2004	-412.7
2005	-318.3
2006	-248.2
2007	-162
2008	-410*

*White House estimate

estimated Congress spends $1.38. Some economists put the number even higher. Fiscal responsibility seems to disappear once the Potomac River is crossed, as neither the executive nor the legislative branch of the federal government has much interest in curbing deficit spending. Sometimes they talk about reducing the *percentage* of increase, but that's about it. We seem to forget that for every dollar of debt we take on, we create an interest obligation that does not go away.

Just take a look at the two graphs on the following page that conservatively predict the continuing decline of the U.S. government's balance sheet. In the first one, you can see that the deficit is heading toward a half trillion dollars and beyond by the end of this decade. In the second, you can see that the deficit as a percentage of the gross domestic product is rising as well.

Mortgaging Our Country to Foreign Countries

Probably the most disturbing aspect of the U.S. government's skyrocketing deficits is that we've financed our healthy economy with debt purchased primarily by foreign governments. Foreign holdings of U.S. Treasury securities, led by Japan ($580.9 billion) and China (386.8 billion), now total $2.34 trillion, representing more than forty-four percent of our public debt.[14] If Japan and China ever lost faith in our economy and sold their U.S. securities, we would be faced with an economic crisis.

This is not so farfetched. As President George W. Bush began simultaneously cutting taxes and increasing spending, the International Monetary Fund (IMF) issued a report stating that with our rising budget deficit and ballooning trade imbalance, the United States is running up a foreign debt of such record-breaking proportions that it threatens the financial stability of the global economy. It warned that our large budget deficits pose "significant risks" and that within a few years the United States' net financial obligations to the rest of the world could represent forty percent of our total economy, creating "an unprecedented level of external debt for a large industrial country" that could play havoc with the value of the dollar and international exchange rates.

14 As of November 2007 according to the U.S. Treasury Department

U.S. Government Surpluses and Deficits 1970-2010

SOURCE: OFFICE OF MANAGEMENT AND BUDGET

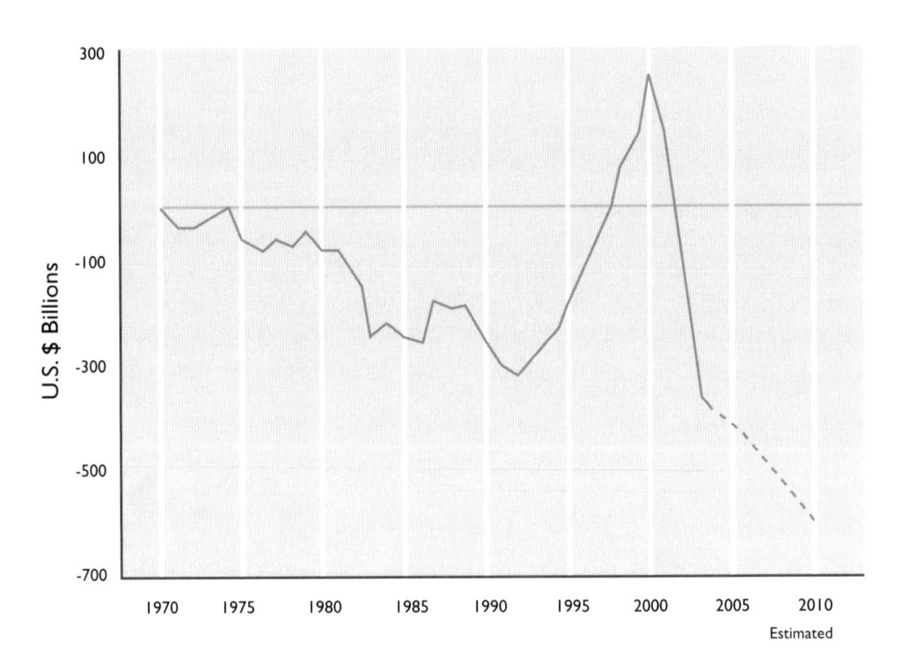

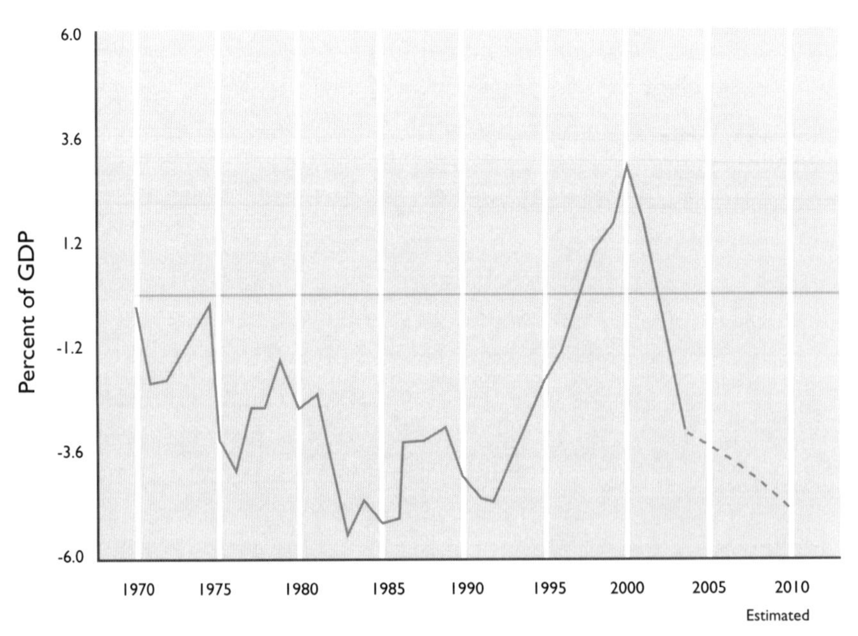

The politicians in Washington, both Republicans and Democrats, appear to believe the federal government can borrow ever-more increasing sums because we will always be able to tap foreign creditors in order to finance our deficit. But on our current trajectory, there will inevitably come a time when our foreign friends will tell us politely that we are no longer creditworthy.

If I Were a Corporation

Imagine if I were the chairman of a large public corporation that not only was losing money, but declared it would continue to lose money for the foreseeable future. What if I announced that through a comprehensive course of cost reduction, the company would be able to break even by the third year, but that management had rejected this strategy? What if I further declared that large expense categories, such as material, labor, burden, and general and administrative costs, could not be touched under any circumstances? You would think I had taken leave of my senses and would call for my resignation.

Yet that is precisely how our federal government operates. If the U.S. government were a corporation and continued to mismanage its finances year after year, it would be forced to declare bankruptcy. Creditors and shareholders would refuse to support an organization which for fifty years had set records for outspending its receipts. A company like that would be broken up; its assets sold off to try to satisfy its debts. But when our president, his executives and cabinet officers, and both houses of Congress act in the same manner, no one raises an alarm.

Is it really too much to ask for the federal government to apply the same fiscal philosophy and be held to the same financial standards as public corporations? Shareholders expect those in charge to keep their interests in mind when making financial decisions. They expect management to keep debt under control, to spend less than they take in, and to set realistic goals while keeping the welfare of the corporation in mind. Citizens of the United States should expect nothing less from our elected leaders. We should insist that the federal government apply the same straightforward fiscal philosophy to its own finances that shareholders expect from public corporations.

Unfortunately, for fifty years our federal government has done just the opposite. It has been piling up debt at a furious pace in a pell-mell rush toward runaway deficits that can only lead to fiscal disaster. We have become a country of double standards, one for businessmen, the other for politicians. In a few decades, we have gone from being the world's largest creditor to the world's largest debtor, and our trade balance has gone from a surplus to a monumental deficit. In the process, our government has placed itself in a position that could allow foreign nations to influence policy under the threat that they will stop buying our debt. Should foreign lenders decide to act on that threat, our entire way of life would be threatened. Once the percentage of foreign holdings of U.S. debt reaches fifty percent, it will likely be too late to reverse the trend. According to the straight line graph below, that will occur in about 2010.

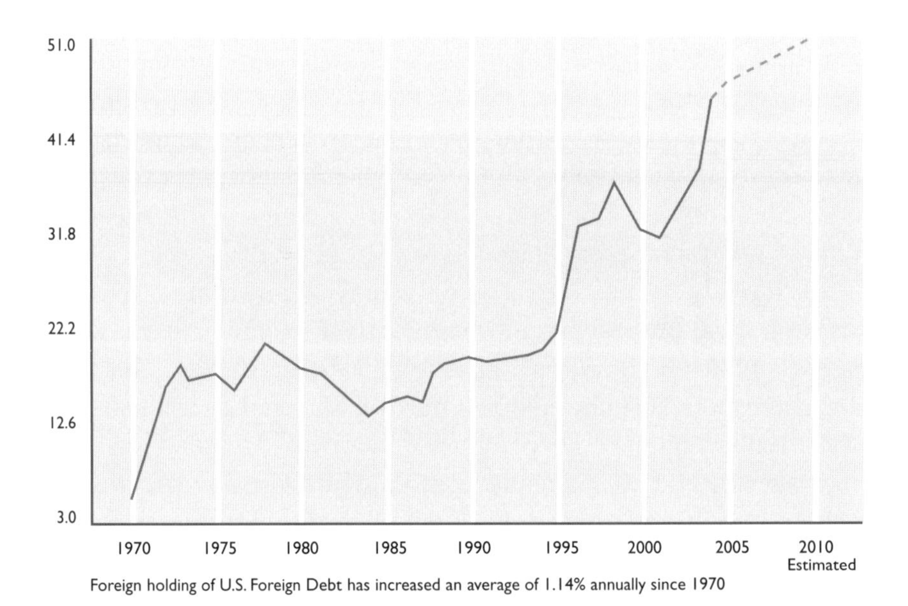

It Has Happened Elsewhere

There is no reason to think that the United States can become the first country in world history to successfully manage its economy by relying on the resources of other countries to finance its excesses. That governments cannot continue to spend beyond their means indefinitely without suffering terrible consequences is a lesson I first learned during World War II, when I brought home 50 million and 10 million mark notes issued by the German Weimar Republic. They were souvenirs, worthless as currency, remnants of what happened between the World Wars when Germans would take baskets of these bills down to the store to buy groceries.

The same thing happened much more recently in Latin America. In fact, Figgie International was so concerned about the double digit inflation the United States weathered in the 1970s that it commissioned a study to investigate how businesses in South America coped with high inflation. At the time, countries like Brazil and Bolivia were experiencing up to triple-digit inflation. In one four-month period Bolivia's currency was debased 10,000 times—one million percent. Cash that had been worth $5,000 was worth fifty cents.

We also looked at Argentina, perhaps the best example of a once mighty economy demolished by runaway inflation. From the early 1900s until about 1950 Argentina was a global economic power—the fifth most productive nation in the world. After a long period of hyperinflation, its financial status deteriorated, and in 2001 it announced the largest debt default in history. Argentina is still struggling to recover.

We go blindly along thinking the same thing can't happen in the United States, but it can because we are looking at problems we have never seen before. We are seeing disaster coming at us with the speed of lightning and we are mesmerized by it. If the wheels don't come off in the form of a severe and sudden depression, then we must accept that the most logical scenario is runaway inflation sometime in the next two decades. We were told unequivocally by economists, corporate leaders, and bankers in Argentina, Brazil, and Bolivia that the U.S. government is following a path leading to runaway inflation, just as their governments did. In fact, one banker posited that the United States was following the same path as had Argentina, but that we were thirty years behind them. That was about fifteen years ago.

> We talk about loaded guns in this country. Loaded government printing presses are far more deadly. We have become a massive zero coupon bond.

We Have Seen the Enemy and It Is Us

While it is easy to blame our legislators for allowing deficits to spiral out of control, we, the people, must accept an equal share of the blame. Washington has become captive to special interest groups of all sizes, each demanding their own piece of the pie. But we all belong to one or more of these special interest groups, each with its hand stretched outward. There was a time in our history when we were proud to say, "I am an American." We thought and acted like Americans, and worried about what was good for the country. Today it seems as if we are no longer Americans first, but rather members of highly vocal special interest groups that don't worry much about the overall health of the country.

President Kennedy, in his inaugural speech said, "Ask not what your country can do for you—ask what you can do for your country." It is time we all took that sentiment to heart. Have we become so selfish that we will allow this great republic to disintegrate before our very eyes? As a country, we have one last shot at achieving fiscal sanity, but it must be done quickly. We have it within our power to be cost conscious, responsible, and steadfast—or we can continue along our current road to disaster. Twenty years ago I was one of the many co-chairs of President Reagan's Private Sector Survey on Cost Control, called the *Grace Commission*, after its chairman, J. Peter Grace. Organized into three dozen task forces chaired by 161 top executives from around the country and staffed by more than 2,000 volunteers, the Grace Commission came up with 2,500 recommendations to cut costs in every part of the U.S. budget that, if implemented, would have saved $1.9 trillion annually by the year 2000. Unfortunately, our suggestions were ignored by Congress. But these same cuts, and then some, could easily be identified today by a Grace Commission-type investigation.

We are on a fast track to perdition unless the leaders of our country get together to agree that debt and deficit are serious problems and that getting the country into fiscal balance is a top priority. I know what can happen to a company, and a country, that spends its way to oblivion. I also know the tremendous opportunities that a healthy U.S. economy can provide. I choose door number two. So should you.

Afterword

HARRY E. FIGGIE Jr.

Matthew and I are again on the lookout for companies we can improve and grow, and build into something larger and more vibrant than their individual parts.

I FEEL SO FORTUNATE to live in a country that gave me the opportunity to start with next to nothing, and to build something of value. I wrote this book not only to explain how I did it, but also to demonstrate how someone could just as easily do it today. There was no blueprint when I began growing Automatic Sprinkler forty-five years ago. But many people have built businesses from scratch without a blueprint. My way is just one.

There is, however, a single common denominator of any method used to grow a company. They all need an environment, created by policies promoted by the federal government, that encourages small businesses, the engine that drives our economy. According to the U.S. Small Business Administration, companies with fewer than 500 employees employ about half of all private sector employees, pay more than 45 percent of total U.S. private payroll, and generate sixty to eighty percent of new jobs annually.

Fortunately, the opportunity still exists in this country to build a billion dollar company from scratch. According to the U.S. Census

Bureau's Statistics of U.S. Businesses, more than ninety-seven percent of all companies in the United States have under $50 million in sales. Many of these can be bought and used as a launching pad to grow a much larger business. In fact, nowhere else, and at no other time in human history, has it been easier for entrepreneurs to locate the right companies, find the necessary seed money, and create something out of nothing. That was America in 1963, and it is even more so America in 2008 and beyond. Remember, in 1963 money was much tougher to come by, as pension funds were in their infancy and it was difficult to use bank loans to acquire companies.

On a personal note, it is exhilarating to see this building process firsthand with the next generation. My entrepreneurial optimism is piqued as I watch my son Matthew use many of the principles outlined in this book to create his own set of building blocks and begin to mold them into large, diversified operations. Like a flashback to the 1960s, Matthew and I are on the lookout for companies in multiple industries that we can improve and grow and that can be built into something larger and more vibrant than their individual parts.

Yet even as Matthew follows my blueprint, there are a few subtle differences. He is not, for example, rolling every company we acquire into a single public entity. And because Matthew has a much more extensive financial background than I ever did, we are simultaneously building a diversified, mutli-disciplined investment company charged with certain targeted strategies, such as providing seed capital for new nucleuses and financing additional "tuck-in" acquisitions.

Matthew has long stated that the final chapter of Figgie International has yet to be written. The new operations will look very different from the public entity that I ran for thirty years. But certain principles—like cost reductions to maximize profitability and increase cash flow, a balance between internal and external growth, creating and maintaining an entrepreneurial culture, the nucleus theory, and focused growth strategies—will never go out of style. I truly hope that in another forty years Matthew, and many of you, will be able to say the same thing about this book.

Index

P

R

S

T

U

V

W